The
Architect
of Eden

The
Architect
of Eden

J. SCOTT CATRON

WESTBOW
PRESS
A DIVISION OF THOMAS NELSON

WestBow Press books may be ordered through booksellers or by contacting:

WestBow Press
A Division of Thomas Nelson
1663 Liberty Drive
Bloomington, IN 47403
www.westbowpress.com
1-(866) 928-1240

Because of the dynamic nature of the Internet, any web addresses or links contained in this book may have changed since publication and may no longer be valid. The views expressed in this work are solely those of the author and do not necessarily reflect the views of the publisher, and the publisher hereby disclaims any responsibility for them.

Certain stock imagery © Thinkstock.
Any people depicted in stock imagery provided by Thinkstock are models, and such images are being used for illustrative purposes only.

C. Lee Chandler, III Editor
Jason Smith Cover Artist

ISBN: 978-1-44973-600-2 (e)
ISBN: 978-1-4497-3601-9 (sc)
ISBN: 978-1-4497-3602-6 (hc)

Library of Congress Control Number: 2011963620

Printed in the United States of America

WestBow Press rev. date: 01/10/2012

Contents

Preface

In the fall of 1994, I found myself at a monumental crossroads in my life. I was on a four-nation missionary tour of Southeast Asia, but most of my mind and emotions were still back at home. Many years of very diverse ministry had culminated into one big question mark as I pondered, "Who am I, and where do I go from here?" One evening, while praying in my hotel room in Ghanzou, China, the Spirit of God began to speak some strange directions into my heart. Months of spiritual turmoil and wondering seemed to be culminating into an answer I did not expect to hear. It sounded like God wanted me leave and plant a church in my hometown.

Let me be clear here—at this point, my ministry experiences had taken me from Christian rock-n-roll to leading worship on the shores of multiple nations. I was very comfortable being in the spotlight and ministering before crowds of any size. I loved God, and I loved ministry. But just to be honest, I actually felt sorry for pastors. I thought they had drawn the short straw and were stuck with the least-desirable ministry position available in the body of Christ. Those who were more fortunate got to travel and do the proverbial, "Blow in, blow up, and blow out." As a traveling minister, I had the luxury of entertaining the illusion that wherever I went, people would be radically changed. Pastors, on the other hand, were stuck with the same old bunch of people week after week. They daily faced the sad reality of laboring with people who did not want to change—that is, of course, until one of us highly anointed road warriors blew into town for a couple of days. No, pastoring could not be my lot. In fact, I had emphatically declared it would be a cold day in hell before I would become a pastor.

Along with the fact God had obviously gotten His wires crossed somewhere when He called me to be a pastor, I also had solid reasons to challenge Him on the "hometown" part of His misguided call. I knew that the last thing my hometown of Princeton, West Virginia, needed was another church. You couldn't sling a dead cat in that town without it getting hung up on a steeple somewhere. I continued praying about it, even entertaining the idea that this was all just a fiendish satanic plot to derail my true calling from God. I entered warfare mode and pretty much rebuked every devil within ten city blocks of my hotel. But even with the darkness dispelled and the hordes of hell on the run … nothing changed. Suffice it to say, by the time I returned home that fall, it was very clear to me that it truly was the Spirit of God speaking to my heart. God had indeed called me to plant a new church in my hometown.

In May of 1995, my wife and I planted a church called Cornerstone Family Church. We recently celebrated sixteen years of ministry, and God has indeed proven that He was not out of His mind when He spoke to my heart. Even though there is indeed an abundance of churches in Princeton, the vision God placed in my heart has by no means been a reproduction of anything that previously existed there. Our contemporary style of fishing for men has landed a harvest of young, un-churched families that may have never darkened a church door if not for this work. We have learned to present the gospel to a slice of our culture that might have never heard or understood it if Cornerstone Family Church did not exist. In the process, God has taught me how to break the norms of tradition and become a pastor (though a very unconventional one) to His people.

This experience of responding to the call of God's Spirit has taught me to stop trusting my human understanding and to lean more on His. As a result, when this same familiar voice recently began to speak to me about writing a book—well, my first carnal response was, "Do we really need another Christian book?" The market seems so flooded to me, with endless numbers of books on every topic that you can imagine and a few topics that seem a little too imagined—if you know what I mean.

I get it, though; God's ways are not our ways. I am not a writer, and I'm not sure how many more books need to be written, but I am going to be obedient and let this thing unfold, believing there is a need and a purpose in it that is bigger than me. I believe this may be one of those times when I need to take something that's already been done, do it in a different way, and let God reach some folks who have never been reached before.

I do know that as every expanding generation walks with God, there is an ever-expanding revelation of who God is, what He wants from us, and how this whole thing with Him is supposed to work. As church history progresses, it is easy to see a sanctification process playing out in our theological and experiential connection with God. Despite our tendency to cling to the faith of our grandfathers, the progressive truths of God continue to reveal themselves to those who hunger and seek for truth.

My prayer is that when you finish this book, a whole bunch of stuff is going to make sense to you that might not have before. I pray that the complex is made simple and the instructions of God suddenly seem very doable. Go brew yourself a good pot of coffee, turn your cell phone off, and let me take you on a little journey into the heart and the mind of the Architect of Eden.

Acknowledgments

I'd like to give some special thanks to those who held my hands high through many years leading to the writing of this book.

First, to my wonderful wife of twenty-eight years—through the highs and lows of marriage and ministry, you have demonstrated what covenant was meant to be. Your sacrifice and support through this rollercoaster life we have shared has been the underlying strength to everything I've ever succeeded at. The two have become one, and any fruit that may ever come from this book is ours to share together.

To my beautiful daughter, Hannah. For many years, I have preached the heart of God as our Father, but it was not until you came along that I truly understood the depth of His love for us. You have been the living object lesson that has guided me deeper into the mind of God. The more time you and I spend together, the more I can relate to the relationship our heavenly Father wants with us. Thanks for allowing Daddy to cancel a couple fishing trips to get this book knocked out. You will also share in any fruit of this work with Mommy and me.

To my dad, who is no longer with us, and my mom, who is still kicking high at eighty-nine. It is the ground you plowed in me the first eighteen years of my life that prepared me for any harvest to follow. Thanks for making me go to church, get up on a stage in front of people, and go to Bible college. You are proof that parents know more than kids think they know.

And last, to my awesome church family at Cornerstone Family Church in Princeton, West Virginia. You have allowed the material of this book to be tried out on you first. You are not just my congregation but my partner in all we put our hands to together. Iron has sharpened iron, and as one, we have accomplished this feat. Thanks for your willingness to share me with a cause much bigger than ourselves. You guys rock!

Introduction

A Pastor's Opening Thoughts

I remember the story of a young man who once asked an older pastor about his sermon preparation time. He asked the pastor how long it took to prepare a fifteen-minute sermon. The pastor responded that it would take him all week. With eyebrows lifted, the young man then asked how long it would take to preach an hour-long message. The older pastor chuckled a little and said, "Oh, I'm ready for that right now." His point was, it's much harder to make things concise and to the point than to expand on a topic.

I realize that most of the short chapters in this book are topics that could easily become books within themselves—and to tell you the truth, they are subjects that need to be expanded on. But every book has a purpose and a hope. With this book, my hope is to stimulate your thinking and to draw some folks out of the small boxes they tend to live in and introduce them to the bigger world of God. It's what I believe to be an ice-breaker into deeper and clearer revelation that is beginning to flood the hearing of God's people.

I understand that some of the content of this book kicks hard against the grain of twentieth-century church ideologies. But church history confirms over and over again that the body of Christ never grows unless we're challenged in ways that stir our emotions and force us to confront our theology. Thank God we are at least past the days of burning people at the stake for deviating from church norms … right?

Here's my advice for those of you who were kind enough to take the time to read this book. Use it more like a daily devotional. Take individual chapters on holiness or godliness and give God *some time* to work it into your life. Use the book as a blueprint—a manual, if you will—to very contemplative and intentional seasons of growth in your life. Don't throw the baby out with the bathwater. Some parts may quickly inspire or direct you while other parts might make you mad enough to slap me into next week. For the parts that instantly resonate—set up camp there for a while. For the parts that aren't clicking, save them for another day.

I do know this: the truth really will set you free. It will set you free to *be* who God made you to be, and that's all I really want this book to accomplish.

Chapter 1

The Art of Seeing God

It was 1992, and communism had just fallen in Russia. I was fortunate to be part of one of the first crusade teams to get into Russia to hold evangelistic services and help plant new churches. It was my first time out of the United States and in a culture where I had to adapt to a language barrier. Spending three weeks with our interpreter helped me to pick up on a few simple words though. I learned just enough to buy a Coke and thank the people who sold it to me. However, there was a big difference in memorizing a few common catchphrases and actually being able to sit down and have a comprehensible conversation with one of the wonderful people of Russia. Because I did not truly understand the language, I was often left bewildered at what in the world was going on around me.

During my last sixteen years as a pastor, I have noticed that my situation in Russia clearly mirrors a problem we face in the body of Christ today. We have memorized a bunch of Christian catchphrases and may even be able to recite definitions for many of the common biblical terms. But does that equate to understanding the language of God? We struggle to read biblical passages in context, which is the main reason why there are so many different movements and denominations in Christianity today. When we fail to see God's redundancy in patterns and systems, we grossly complicate the Bible. People are overwhelmed by trying to learn the thousands of different things they think God was trying to say in the Bible instead of simply hearing the few important points He was trying to make.

King Solomon once stated in his great collection of Proverbs, "For lack of vision [revelation], God's people perish" (Prov. 29:18 KJV). The context is clear. Because God's people could not SEE what God needed for them to *see*, they could not be what He wanted them to be. It's simple; your purpose and destiny in God will be completely limited to the degree that you understand what God is trying to tell you.

Obviously there is a great deal of confusion in what various schools of thought believe they *see* in the Bible. We're all over the place with our doctrines and what we *think* God is up to. The disparity and extremes between various denominations and movements is incredible, to say the least. Can everybody be right? Hmmm, could everybody be wrong? Maybe everyone has a piece of the truth—but which piece is the right piece?

Well, I sure do not claim to have a lock on truth, but I absolutely understand where the breakdown in finding truth often takes place. It's in the simple understanding that God is spirit. Because God is spirit, His words are—wait, it's coming—*spiritual!* We, on the other hand, are not like God. We are carnal creatures with carnal minds. Carnal simply means natural, so our first response to God's words is to try and naturalize them in a way that makes sense to the carnal mind. That's why the apostle Paul said that we must have our minds made new. He went on to say, in Romans 12:2, that having this "new" mind would be the *only* way to know God's plan for our lives.

This language barrier between God and man is most clearly seen in the interaction between Jesus and … well, whoever He was talking to. Not only did He re-translate almost every single Scripture

He quoted, but He also couldn't seem to say anything without his followers going, "Huh?"

Jesus would say things like, "If a man wants to *see* the kingdom of God, he must be born again." Nicodemus, a really smart guy, could not understand what Jesus was saying. While his carnal mind was struggling to reason out the biological aspects of Jesus' comment, he missed the whole point of what Jesus was trying to say. Ironically enough, Jesus was telling Nicodemus that unless he took on a new mind, he would never *see* (or understand) God's plan.

Jesus declared, "Tear this temple down, and I'll rebuild it in three days" (John 2:19 KJV). Oh my goodness, what a stink that stirred up. The disciples could not *see* that Jesus was talking about His death and resurrection. The good news is that these very same disciples did begin to take on new minds, and they did begin to understand the language of God. Just weeks after that whole "tear this temple down" debacle, Peter was out in the middle of Main Street Jerusalem quoting the prophet Joel. He was quoting things about the sun being darkened, the moon turning to blood, and all kinds of crazy stuff. The context of this great passage from Joel was in reference to the baptism of the Holy Spirit that had just been poured out on the 120 as they tarried in the upper room, which is recorded in the book of Acts. Wow, I'm surprised that somebody didn't think that the passage in Joel 2 was talking about nuclear holocaust. Wait a minute—they did. Several twentieth-century Christian novelists did just that, despite the fact that Peter already explained this as something spiritual.

Jesus proved we don't understand the language of God—not until our minds are renewed (and that process takes time, just like learning any language). But learning the language of God—to truly *see* what God is trying to show us—will require us to "cast down imaginations and every high thing we've exalted above the knowledge of God" (2 Cor. 10:5). These images we've erected with our carnal minds are blocking us from seeing what God really needs us to see. Without this vision to see what God is saying, our very purpose and birthright will perish.

There is an art and a spiritual science, if you will, to understanding what God has been trying to say to us from the beginning. It is true that the Bible declares that this message from God has been hid from the carnally wise. However, Paul declares emphatically in 1 Corinthians 2:9–10, "No eye has seen, no ear has heard, no mind has conceived what God has prepared for those who love Him. But God *has* revealed it to us *by His Spirit*. The Spirit searches *all* things, even the deep things of God." God *wants* you to see some stuff.

We should cry out in agreement with the apostle Paul as he prayed, "That the eyes of your heart may be enlightened in order that you may *know* the hope to which He has called you, the riches of His glorious inheritance in the saints ..." (Eph. 1:18). It is a prayer that should be answered in you and me right here, right now. It is not for me to see someday in the sweet by and by; I need to see it now. It is not when we all get to heaven that we will need to understand the Kingdom of God; it is right here, right now. We need to understand the language of God today. We can open up the Bible and clearly see what His Spirit is trying to say to us. My reward may very well be down the road in an age to come, but my *purpose* and reason for being are *now*.

Our Father wrote us a letter. This letter contains everything we might ever need to know about how to live life to its fullest, to walk with Him in true relationship, and in the process, to rule and reign in the earth like kings. But if we can't decipher the language of God, we will not only mistranslate His Word into the fodder of religion, but we will also complicate it to the point of making sure that even those who follow such a religion can't agree on its precepts.

God is spirit; His words are spiritual. I pray that as you continue to read, His Spirit will help you to learn his language so you can learn how He does things. His ways are not our ways, but that does not mean you can't learn those ways—if you know what He's saying.

Chapter 2

The Unrolling of the Blueprint

Repetition of familiar imagery is one of the primary keys God uses in the Bible to help us *see* what He's talking about. God takes things we have learned to relate to over generations of cultural existence and uses them to represent what He wants and to show us how He operates. Using these types, patterns, shadows, symbols, and allegorical pictures helps us to translate the language of God.

Some common examples include the redundant usage of words like *family*, *sons*, or *bride* to describe who we are to God. Repetition translates into an understanding of intimacy that God wants with us. The repetitive imagery of things like gold and fire helps us to see the process that God is using to turn us into something valuable and beautiful. The redundant use of certain numbers in Scripture, within context, begins to speak of the work of God in ways that become very clear to the reader.

God uses this same pattern of speaking to help us relate to who He is. Our human experience helps us relate to God when He refers to Himself as a father, a brother, or a friend. When God speaks of Himself with such specific terminology, we understand that our whole connection with Him will depend on our understanding of each descriptive term.

When Jesus, God in flesh, came to the earth, it is not an insignificant detail that His profession was as a carpenter. There is little doubt that Jesus would have culturally followed in His earthly father's footsteps to carry out the family vocation. It was a skill set that not only lent to working with wood but also with stones. From this place of experience, Jesus would speak about building your house properly on the rock so it could withstand storms. From that understanding of who Jesus was, Peter would later refer to Him as being the chief cornerstone and talk about how He was carving us as living stones and fitting us together as a house. God, through the expression of His Son, Jesus, found identity in the earth as a builder. This description is a key to our understanding of God.

Understanding the Bible, however, is always limited to those things we culturally relate with. God, usually playing off of things common to the Hebrew culture, used imagery that often held deeper meaning that we pass through the filter of our culture. A case in point is the Greek word *tekton,* translated as *carpenter* when referring to Jesus' family vocation. *Tekton* did not only refer to one who had the hands of a builder but the mind of one also. Simply put, carpenters were often pretty good engineers as well. They didn't just know how to follow the blueprints; they were often the architect of the blueprints.

This picture of God as architect is clearly seen early and often in the Bible as He meticulously unfolded a detailed blueprint for Noah to build the ark and for Moses to build the tabernacle. The stories of God that involve details of construction blanket the Old Testament. From the building of Solomon's Temple to the rebuilding of the walls of Jerusalem after Babylonian captivity to the building of the New Jerusalem in Revelation, God revealed His mode of operation. King David, a man after God's own heart, became a builder. King David's son Solomon followed in the footsteps of his natural as well as his heavenly father as he became a builder. Through that heart of wisdom, King Solomon declared in Psalm 127:1, "Unless the Lord builds the house, its builders labor in vain."

We understand that there is a clear foreshadowing of this carpenter-architect-blueprint thing going on in the Bible. God wants us to see how detailed He is when He builds something. The ark—detailed blueprints. The tabernacle—detailed blueprints. Humans—well, that's the part I'm afraid we may have missed. You see, long before God gave a detailed blueprint for the ark or the tabernacle, He unrolled a very detailed blueprint on how to build *humans*. I'm not talking about the natural part so much. We know how He did that: from the dust of the earth. I'm talking about the *spiritual* parts of human beings. We must remember the words of the great French Jesuit priest, Pierre Teilhard de Chardin, "We are not humans having a spiritual experience, (but) we are spiritual beings having a human experience." With that being said, we must look back into the mirror of God and remember who we are: those made in God's image. God is spirit…and so are we.

Right out of the gate, the first thing God does in His Word is to unroll the blueprint to build a person. It's the first thing He chose to show us. Now think about that for just a moment. We know the Bible is not written in a chronological order, yet through the inspiration of the Holy Spirit, it was recorded and collected in such a way that God made sure our "Genesis," our beginning, would be the first thing we would read. I am sure there is a priority in God's heart for the order in which His Word was given to us. I would even go so far as to say that there is such a priority to God's order in giving us His Word that unless we understand the first thing He says, what follows may be grossly misunderstood.

The first information God tells us ends up being the most important. It is the original blueprint to build our lives in a way that will lead to a beautiful and productive world of ruling, reigning, and walking with God. It is a blueprint with very specific detail and order. If the order is missed, what God is building will not stand;

it will not function correctly, and it certainly will never fulfill the purpose God had in mind.

The blueprint of God unrolled in the creation story of Genesis is methodically ordered. This order or sequence of God is what we call government. God plays off of this term as Old Testament prophets begin to announce the coming of the Messiah, Jesus. Isaiah 9:6–7 says, "For to us a child is born, to us a son is given, and the *government* will be on his shoulders. And He will be called Wonderful Counselor, Mighty God, Everlasting Father, Prince of Peace. Of the increase of his *government* and peace there will be no end." As verse 7 continues, the word kingdom is then interjected, helping us to correlate the two terms. *Government* and *kingdom* speak to the same end: order. So when the many prophecies of Jesus are fulfilled by His coming, it's interesting that He came preaching "the Kingdom of Heaven is at hand."

Oh, how we've turned that phraseology into such a mystery. Some generations of the church have been so mystified by this "kingdom stuff" that we have vilified people who tried to preach a "kingdom message," often even calling them heretics. We still fear what we do not understand, but the mystery really isn't a mystery if you understand the language of God. God's Kingdom is simply God's government. Government is simply an order to how things are done. When Jesus came preaching "the kingdom of God, or heaven, is at hand," it was simply the cry that echoed the words of the prophet Isaiah. When Jesus came, He came to restore order—God's order. This government was on His shoulders. As His order/government increased, so would the peace that comes with it.

Let's make it really simple. I believe the creation account, in the natural, really happened the way the Bible says. It's the starting point of our Christian faith. But following the pattern of Jesus' allegorical style of speaking, we also can see this story is also very spiritual beyond that. The creation story is an ordered blueprint for humanity. It's the ordered steps of a righteous man that the psalmist spoke of centuries later. It's God's government—His kingdom—that was established from the beginning … before man lost the blueprint. Jesus came to restore the blueprint and help us to follow it again.

It was the apostle Paul who explained the biblical concept of natural realities representing spiritual ones. He said, "The spiritual did not come first, but the natural, and after that the spiritual" (1 Cor. 15:46). He emphasized that the stories of old, which we call the Old Testament, were given to teach us the spiritual lessons of God. The story of creation is both natural and spiritual. Most biblical pictures that follow the creation story are simply a redundant look at the same blueprint using different symbolism. Whether referring to the building of the tabernacle of Moses or John's new Jerusalem, it's all repetitive of the original blueprint. The blueprint is simply the design for mankind. It's a picture of what the Creator originally wanted us to look like and the instructions for how to build it.

I have heard Myles Monroe, the great Bahamian pastor and writer, say many times that if you want to know how something is supposed to work, then you have to go ask the one who made it. That's what this book is about: going back to the front of the manual (page one of the blueprint). We're going back to the architect Himself and saying, "Show us how this thing is supposed to work."

Chapter 3

The Logo of God

Ten years after planting Cornerstone Family Church, we faced a major step in our faith. We had outgrown our existing facility, and we saw an opportunity to buy the land beside us where we could build a new, contemporary structure. Boy, what a process! I had some previous carpentry experience and had even built my first house, but I had no idea about the red tape involved in a project like this. The endless acquiring and satisfying of legal permits and codes was exhausting. The final document that contained all the information that was necessary to satisfy the stringent requirements to build our church the right way was called the architectural blueprints.

I felt very important when I got my own personal copy of the blueprints, though I must admit I really wasn't qualified to read most of it. But the first page—well, that page I understood. It was simple and only had a few pieces of information. First, it had an artist's rendition of what the front view of the building would look like, along with the name of the project. It also had an index at the bottom of the page telling you the order of the pages to follow. And last of all, it had a *logo* of the company that drew up the plans. As King Solomon once said, "There's nothing new under the sun"

(Eccl. 1:9). I must tell you, concerning this model for drawing up blueprints, that's entirely true.

Genesis 1:1, the front page of God's blueprint for humanity, says, "In the beginning God created the heavens and the earth." There, within that short verse, we get a visual with the project's name: "heaven and earth." We also get the logo of the architect designing the project: God. Can I show you something really cool? John 1:1—I call it the Jesus version of creation—says, "In the beginning was the Word, and the Word was with God, and the word was God." The term for *Word* in this creation retrospect passage is the Greek word *logos*. It's actually the word from which we get our term *logo*.

Genesis 1:1 is the front page of God's blueprint. It contains the most important information necessary to satisfy all the requirements of the law and the *logo* of the certified architect. The architect identified by the logo knows all the codes and how to fulfill them in the blueprint. The one represented by the logo gives credibility to the plans. God, expressed by John as the person of Jesus Christ, is the author and finisher of this project called heaven and earth—both natural and spiritual. His logo guarantees that the index of building steps following page one will produce a solid, functional structure when completed.

If a blueprint does not display the logo of the architect, the blueprints would not be considered to be legitimate plans. It is the logo—or should I say *logos*—of Genesis 1:1 that legitimizes everything in God's Word that follows. Discarding God as the maker of heaven and earth will create a snowball effect that will roll all the way to the cross. If God is not the architect of creation in the way Genesis says, then the rest of the Bible is null and void. If God is not the architect of humanity, then everything the Bible promises (including eternal life) is a fairy tale, and our lives suddenly mean very little. If Genesis 1:1 is not the truth, then what is? If God is not the Creator, then there is no higher power in control, and we are on our own. You tell me, is that not the most despairing and scary thing you can imagine?

If Genesis is true, then everything that follows it is true. If the front page of the blueprint is accurate and God did create it all— well, everything that follows suddenly carries great weight. If God is the architect and Creator of it all, then only He knows how it is all supposed to work. Humanity is clearly subject to God's order if humanity desires God's promises.

It all begins and ends with God. He is the Alpha and the Omega. All we see and know was created by Him and for Him. He had in His mind what the project would look like before construction ever began. He understood the purpose of the finished work before the blueprint was ever unrolled. He and He alone designed the index of steps that would follow as creation began to unfold.

In the beginning ... *God!* If you believe that and accept that, then you must accept the building stages that follow for humanity. You must begin to see divine design as the pages of His blueprint are put into motion. Page one makes it all official; His logo has been stamped upon its pages.

The architectural logo has legitimized the complete blueprint. With that code satisfied, let the project begin.

Chapter 4

Beauty out of Ashes

Who can really say with any certainty what happened prior to Genesis 1:2 in universal history—prior to God creating the earth as we presently know it? What we do know from Scripture, though, is a somewhat gray presentation of the conditions that existed when God started creating our world. The God-inspired word Moses uses to describe the starting point is the Hebrew word *tohu,* which means empty, formless, useless, confused, ruined, without purpose, and *chaotic.* Wow! That's a pretty dismal picture. On top of that, the Bible goes on to say that darkness was over the surface of the deep.

When I was younger, I would try to imagine what all of this meant in the natural world. I would picture swirling gas clouds and meteors running amok as they crashed into things. Of course, whatever I pictured is probably just as accurate—or not—as anybody else's picture. But when we look past the natural and into the spiritual imagery here, the details of Moses' description become much more relatable. We see a record of life's starting point for not just the earth but also those things made from the dust of that earth. We see the condition of any human life prior to having an encounter with God. It's a picture of humanity before it encounters the voice of God or is touched by God. It's a picture of a life that is empty and has no purpose. It's a story of darkness, depression, and complete chaos. It's the first time, with spiritual ears, that we hear humanity say things like, "I just feel so empty inside. I'm confused. What's my purpose? Who am I? I feel like there's a dark cloud over my life. I'm so depressed, and I don't know why. My life is in shambles, and I just don't know where to go from here. Everything is so chaotic in my life that I simply don't know where to start to get it on track." Do these statements sound familiar? They are the cry of those made from the dust of the earth who have not yet made a personal connection with the one who created them. As a pastor, these are the statements I hear from people almost every week.

Genesis 1:2 is the natural starting point to every human life. Some humans listen to the voice of their Creator early and forego some of the darkness and chaos of life. Many others only cry out from their depressed, empty places after desperation has finally driven them to seek what's spiritually missing from their lives. However, no matter how you slice this thing, *tohu* describes life outside of God to a tee.

It does seem quite incredible that when you look at the end of God's little construction project, you end up with one of the most beautiful sights one can ever imagine. From emptiness, darkness, and chaos, God still found enough building material to complete a work we call the Garden of Eden. This architect—this carpenter—seems to really have a knack for bringing beauty out of ashes, as the prophet Isaiah would later declare. It just doesn't seem like He needs that much to work with to produce a grand finished product. Somehow, we have to see there is a very intentional message from God in this story. I am convinced that God wants us to see the description of where creation started, to look in the mirror at our own lives, and to know that wherever we're at in life, God can start there. It doesn't matter how messed up we are. It doesn't matter how little there is to work with; it's enough for this very creative builder.

Hebrews 11:2 says, "By faith we understand that the universe was formed at God's command, so that what is seen was not made out of what was visible." The Latin phrase *"ex nihilo"* is drawn from this imagery and simply means that God can create something out of nothing. He proved it through His own flesh and blood, Jesus, time and time again. In fact, Jesus' first recorded miracle was turning water into wine. He took the blandest liquid that existed and made a wine that was declared to be the best those folks had ever tasted! He literally turned the tasteless into the tasteful. Five loaves of bread and two fish was enough to feed thousands when He put His hands on it. Throughout the Bible, God redundantly displays the picture of his *ex nihilo* wonders. A slingshot (1 Sam. 17:50), the jawbone of a donkey (Judges 15:15), and a farmer's ox-goad (Judges 3:31) all became powerful weaponry when they were empowered by God. Miracle after miracle in the Bible began with insufficiency and inadequacy—that is, until God stepped in.

God's blueprint calls for you to be a beautiful garden or a jewel-encrusted city when God gets done with you. But you may say, "Look at my condition." The Architect of Eden would say, "Wherever you are, whatever you have, *it's enough!*" Your condition may blow the minds of your family and even a few counselors, but for God, it's a perfect environment to create.

One man's trash is another man's treasure. It seems like this was the first thing God wanted you to know about yourself. Whoever you are, wherever you've been, whatever you've done ... yeah, He can work with that.

Chapter 5

A Hovering God

The world is dark, empty, useless, formless, and one big, chaotic mess; that's the description of creation's starting point. It may also very well be a fair assessment of where your life is currently. I want to make sure you see what God very intentionally hoped you would see in this passage: there in the darkness, His Spirit was hovering. He wasn't repulsed by the chaos; no, He was hanging out in it.

Boy do I get a front-row seat to see this as a pastor as I watch people struggle with condemnation and worthlessness. These are people who desperately need God to touch their lives but feel too dirty to ask. They are folks who are battling shame, guilt, and a dozen different complexes that all involve God "hating" them.

If we jump ahead in the creation story, we see Adam dealing with his shame by hiding from God in the leaves. He had messed up bad and knew it. Though he had become accustomed to intimately walking with God in the cool of the day, now he was afraid of God and assumed God would want nothing more to do with him. But God did show up after Adam messed up … to walk with him. God knew Adam sinned, yet still He came to spend time with him.

It's like *déjà vu* as we look ahead to the gospel of Luke and see a man named Zacchaeus (Luke 19) wrestling with this same dirty feeling. He was a chief tax collector, which means he was the most-despised kind of man in Hebrew culture. He betrayed his own and became an ambassador of Rome to help pillage the hard-earned wages of Israel. Since there's nothing new under the sun, this dude probably chose his vocation in attempt to counterbalance all of the low self-esteem and many complexes he battled as a very short man. He felt he was "somebody" now. He no doubt enjoyed—at least for a season—being the big shot with authority to even command the Roman soldiers. "Who's laughing now," became his attitude.

As life always shows, there was a price tag to Zacchaeus's decision. Now he was an outcast who had sinned against his own people and therefore against God Himself. When Zacchaeus got news of Jesus coming to town, he was a torn man. He wanted with everything in his heart to get close to this Messiah, this Savior of mankind, but his condemning heart led him to believe that Jesus would hate him, just as the people hated him. Zacchaeus did what Adam did; he hid in the fig leaves. He resolved to simply observe God from a distance—where it was safe. But Jesus knew where Zacchaeus was at, just like God really knew where Adam was when he said, "Adam, where are you?" Jesus stopped at the base of the sycamore-fig tree, looked up at Zacchaeus, and then said the last thing that short man ever expected to hear from God. "Hey, Zacchaeus, come down out of your hiding place. I want to come to your house today." I promise you, Zach was not the only one shocked by Jesus' desire to be close to him; the rest of the crowd was probably downright angry about it.

The woman caught in adultery was shocked that Jesus would save her from those who rightfully, by law, were ready to stone her (John 8). The leper was in disbelief that Jesus would put His hands on his unclean body (Mark 1). Dirty fishermen thought they were hearing things when they received the invitation to come follow Jesus (Mark

1). There's story after story of humanity's uncleanness and God's willingness to still be in proximity to them.

Because I am a pastor and a counselor, I have witnessed over and over again how this carnal perspective of God can become so intertwined in the human psyche. The trickle-down effect leaks into everything, from marriage and parenting to emotional health, simply because we believe God wants nothing to do with us. God knew about this human condition long before humans existed, so He addressed it right away. He wanted us to know that He would be close, even if we thought He would not want to be. His Spirit would be hovering there, in our chaos, in our darkness, hoping to draw us to Himself.

The Bible says, "While we were still sinners, Christ died for us" (Rom. 5:8). Get it? *While* we were sinners! When we hate ourselves for the things we've done, God still loves us and hovers over our lives. When we unfairly hate Him for how things in our life have turned out, He still loves us and is hovering over our emptiness. When our lives are filled with nothing but chaos because we have intentionally rejected God and lived life for ourselves, He still loves us and is hovering over our brokenness.

He is hovering over your life—regardless. Look back on your life. Can you see now that He was always there? He's waiting for a chance to speak to you in a way you will finally hear. He's waiting for a chance to recreate your life. He's hovering and waiting for an opportunity to take all your darkness, emptiness, and chaos and to turn them into something really beautiful. God's whole process of building you into something beautiful hinges on the hovering of His Spirit in your life and your willingness to believe it and receive it.

Chapter 6

Shedding Some Light

"And God said, 'Let there be light,' and there was light, and it was good" (Gen. 1:3). There in the darkness and chaos, the Spirit of God, who had been hovering, saw that the timing and opportunity were right to speak. The first words out of His mouth to creation had to be just right—precise, even—for His building project to get off the ground.

In the natural, Bible-believing scientists use poetic license to speculate as they explain this light. It is often referred to as some type of cosmic afterglow that permeated the whole universe, allowing for a low level of illumination, but that theory doesn't hold a lot of water since that afterglow would depend on the residual light of distant stars. However, not only were our sun and moon not created until day four of creation, but the stars that are scattered throughout the universe were also not created until that day. The fact is there is no solid scientific theory to explain this light God spoke into existence.

But when we unroll the creation story as a spiritual blueprint, God's first step of creation suddenly makes a lot of sense. He began the ordered steps of His architectural plan by simply turning on some construction lights. You see, the Spirit of God wears many hats throughout the Bible. God, who is spirit, is very active and involved in man's life. Prophets and kings alike were very aware of the Spirit of God's work and primarily saw Him as the one who was a "lamp unto their feet and a light unto their path." In other words, they knew God was revealing what needed to be revealed and directing them where they needed to go in life. Jesus called the Holy Spirit the Counselor and the Comforter. However, the heart of how man has generally seen the work of God's Spirit leads us to call Him the great illuminator, or maybe the great revelator. He shines a light on our lives, our paths, and the direction we need to go. He reveals the things we cannot see, whether they be an unseen enemy ready to pounce on us or hidden sin in our lives.

God's building project started where most of our lives do before we allow God to re-create us: full of chaos, emptiness, and darkness. Our lives are so messed up that we don't even know where to begin to try and get things on track, so God teaches us a "first-things-first" lesson in life. God wants us to understand that the starting point has to be simply shining some light on the situation so we can truly see what's what. Without Spirit-induced illumination, we are too quick to think the problem is one thing when it's often something else. If we don't know where to start when getting our lives back on track, we will do one of two things: we will either become so weary battling the chaos and not knowing what to do about it that we will throw in the towel and give up on life, or we will make hasty decisions of change that only make our problems worse. Choices made in darkness never end up well. We would not even begin to think about building a house in the dark, and God wants us to understand that building a life in darkness will not work either.

I have people come to me all the time who want me to help put their lives back together. As they sit across from me, I hear story after story about the brokenness in their marriages, their finances, their emotional health, and … you get it, the list goes on and on. Because of the trickle-down effect of humanity's condition, people honestly don't know where to start when they attempt to heal their lives. It's all just a—well, you saw the original picture God painted. It's an empty, void, chaotic, and depressed mess. How can anyone really know where to start when righting the ship?

The good news is that God knows where to start. You start by having an encounter with the light of the Holy Spirit. The Bible gives us a beautiful story of such an encounter. It was with a man named Saul. He was a very intelligent, religious man who really thought he had his life together. He was a big cheese in Jewish circles and was on a passionate campaign to rid the earth of a terrible disease called the church. The Jesus movement had taken over Jerusalem and begun to spread through the outlying areas. Saul was a cruel man with a Mafia mindset and slept well at night after torturing innocent Christians. One day during his journey of life, Saul had an encounter with light. Out of the light, the voice of Jesus spoke, and Saul was made very aware of his true condition in life (Acts 9). During his encounter with this light, Paul was given direction—or illumination—about what the first step of the rest of his life needed to be. Because light was shed on his life, stages of change followed that re-created Saul's life into something so beautiful that you and I today are still reaping the benefits from it. His name was changed, his life was changed, and the world was changed … and it all started with an encounter with light.

In the spring of 1983, I had my encounter with this light. I grew up in church and knew all about the religious customs and practices of the church, but I was on the run from God, having never had a personal life-changing encounter with Him. My life had slid into a dark, chaotic pit of alcohol, drugs, and a party lifestyle that consumed and owned me. Ironically, I was attending a Bible college in Lakeland, Florida. I was only there—or so I thought—because it was close to the beach and I had my parents' blessing to be there. I was very aware that the Spirit of God was hovering in my dark world, and the internal fight taking place for my soul was ripping my emotions to pieces. As I lay in my dorm room bed at 2:00 a.m., I felt I was about to smother under the weight of my *tohu* condition. I leapt from my bed and proceeded across campus to the school's chapel, which was open all night. I crawled upon the giant stage, laid down face first, and surrendered my life to the voice that was calling me. On that night, I had an incredible encounter with God where He began to shine a light on my life. He began to illuminate my condition in a very non-condemning, loving way. He brought me into a place of personal revelation and helped me see what I needed to do next to step into His plan of re-creation.

That was twenty-eight years ago, almost to the day as I write about it. Following that day was a succession of days where God began to transform my darkness into light, my emptiness into fullness of joy, and my chaos into a fruitful life of ministry—but it all started with an initial encounter with the Spirit of God, His light of truth, and His voice speaking into my heart.

I'm concerned that too many people who call themselves Christians are struggling in life because they've never truly had a life-altering encounter with God. We may have been driven to the altar by the fear of hell or the enticement of heaven, but was it truly because we heard the voice of God speaking into our darkness? We may have repeated one of our American-style, microwave sinner's prayers, but did we have godly sorrow working in our hearts in the way the apostle Paul described? Was it a cry for God to fix our problems that prompted us to "get saved," or was there a true cry for lordship resonating in our soul? Did we really have a conversion experience or just a church experience? Did our encounter with God produce true repentance? Did we turn from our darkness and begin to walk into the light? Did we merely have our names recorded on some local church's membership roll, or did we have a born-again experience that radically changed the direction our lives were going?

The architect of Eden, the builder of humanity, understands better than anyone how you turn chaos into a beautiful garden, and it starts with an encounter with the light of this world: Jesus. If we go into this light, He becomes the door to salvation. Salvation, as the Bible speaks of it, is a process that leads to great fruitfulness, receipt of God's promises, great joy and peace, a mind-blowing inheritance, power, purpose, abundant life … *but* it *all* starts with an encounter with light.

This light of God's Spirit has been hanging out in your darkness, watching for the right opportunity to speak into your life. This enlightenment of God's Spirit will find you where you are, accept you as you are, and begin to light a new path for you, ending in a beautiful garden. Maybe your encounter with this light is taking place right now as you are reading this book. Maybe this is the day you are hearing the voice of God truly speaking into your life for the first time. Well, all I can say is: *go into the light.* Respond to the drawing of God's ever-loving Spirit by getting real with Him. Twenty-eight years ago I simply said to Him, "Here it is! Take my life, and do with it whatever You want. I'm giving it *all* to You." The words of my mouth weren't what changed the direction of my life on that early morning; it was the cry of my heart that God heard and understood, even beyond my words.

God knows your heart today. Respond to His light. Respond to His voice. If you do, you won't believe the days of creation that can follow.

Chapter 7

Rome Wasn't Built in a Day

"And there was evening, and there was morning—the first *day*" (Gen. 1:5).

Day is the most redundant word used in the creation story. Each stage of God's construction project—both natural and spiritual—is identified by this word. The use of this term is obviously used to mark a time span, but even more, it puts a chronological order to specific stages of development. These days of creation literally become the page numbers of God's architectural blueprint.

The Hebrew term translated into "day'" is the word *yom*. It is a word that has caused great controversy in theological circles because of its broad base usage in the Bible. Most often the context of this word clearly represents a twenty-four-hour period of time, but at other times it is used to represent a collection of days or a season of time. For example, the Bible often talks about "the Day of the Lord" in both the Old Testament and the New Testament. We currently are living in one of those "days"; we call it the New Covenant Age, and it (so far) has lasted two thousand years, or roughly 730,000 twenty-four-hour periods.

Using this term in dual way is not just a Hebrew thing, by the way. We do it all the time in our own American culture. Grandpa might be telling stories about how much things have changed since he was a little boy and say something like, "Back in my day, things were much simpler." Just recently, my daughter was complaining about having to go to bed so early on school nights. I told her, "It won't always be this way. One day you'll get to stay up as long as you want." Clearly the context in both statements represents a season of life, and not a twenty-four-hour time span.

Creationists—those who believe the creation story of the Bible is true—have distinct opinions on the context of day in the first chapter of Genesis. Young-earth creationists argue that believing the days of creation were literal twenty-four-hour time spans is essential to our faith. They see a domino effect that could reach all the way to the cross if our faith is not based on six literal days. Old-earth creationists argue that the days of creation were potentially seasons of days that could have lasted for thousands of years. They would use their theory to allow for fossils of dinosaurs and other elements that seem to be much older than six thousand years.

I must tell you, though, that there is a third category of creationists. I'm not sure what to call us, though I'm sure the other creationist groups could offer some suggestions … that we probably couldn't print. This group simply is not sure that the timetable of creation is all that relevant to our faith. The bottom line we build our faith on in this group is found within the truth that God created it all. It is not important how long it took Him to do it. However, even within this group there are several subgroups.

But consider this: what if this is one of those many times when we have argued and divided ourselves over something in the Bible and *everyone* has been so naturally minded that we've missed God's point? What if God's highly important message was not about the accuracy of the time span but simply the fact there had to be a time span? Let me make this really easy. What if God's point was simply this: if you want to take a dark, formless, useless, chaotic mess and turn it into something beautiful, it won't happen overnight?

Many years ago, someone coined the phrase, "Rome was not built in a day." This figure of speech was, of course, referring to the great Roman Empire that was many generations in the making. We use that phrase all the time to remind people they need to be patient when they are waiting on something in their lives to change. As a counselor and a pastor, my biggest problem when I help people is their unrealistic expectations when they want change in their lives. Their problems have taken years to form, yet folks think the solution will be as easy as simply smacking the "easy button" and everything will be all right.

I mostly fault the church for this microwave mindset many Americans have. We read about the instantaneous miracles of the Bible and somehow decide that every problem can be solved with an altar call and a prayer. We swim in the fallout of addictions but are led to believe that waving the magic wand of a sinner's prayer suddenly makes all things new. Marriages, families, finances, mental health, emotions, dreams are all broken over many days, but many are waiting on a miracle that will fix it in one day.

Trust me as a pastor when I say dysfunctional homes and dysfunctional lives are not re-created by instant miracles but through many days and years of godly discipleship. Broken lives do not very often get fixed in a microwave but in the slow cook of God's healing process where, day by day, all things *are* made new. Our lottery ticket mindset is the biggest giant we face in the modern American church. We expect years of bondage, bad choices, and brokenness to be suddenly erased by a simple trip to the mailbox or the purchase of a lottery ticket. And if we don't get these quick, easy fixes in our lives? Well, then we give up, get divorced, get drunk … and in extreme cases, stick a gun in our mouth. We have learned to run from problems instead of facing them. A flight mentality has become a way of life for so many because they can't handle the timetable of change.

I have lost count of so many I have seen walk through the church door, their lives an empty, chaotic mess. Everything from legal troubles to marriage problems led them there. Their thought often was, *If I start going to church, God will fix everything.* The truth is, the Architect of Eden does have a great blueprint to totally recreate their lives, but when His construction project does not happen as speedily as they think, they are gone. He wants to build the people into houses that will stand through the storms, but they just want quick remodels of their existing houses.

I want to be clear that I am a man who believes that the miracle-working power of God is a very real thing for today. I have had instant healings in my body that could not be explained by doctors. I have laid my hands on tumors in others and felt them disappear. I have witnessed multiple things that had no human explanation, yet they happened. However, to apply the instant miracle concept to man's broken condition is to misrepresent of God's Word. Forgiveness of sin is based on the work of the cross and *is* instant, but the restoration and rebuilding of the life of one who has been forgiven takes time. Jesus may have healed sick bodies in a moment, but the healing of a sick soul may take a few *yoms*.

God knows us better than we know ourselves. He knows that for us to have lasting change, it usually can't come too fast. Change is something we can embrace with longevity when that change happens over time—days. But when it comes too fast, we neither appreciate it nor embrace it as our new lifestyle. The pattern of Israel, especially in the wilderness, was that miracle changes may change the moment of what people experience but it doesn't change the people. Our conditions didn't happen overnight, and they will not change overnight.

God is trying to tell us something of utmost importance in His first conversation with us. He's telling us that He can take a dark, ugly life and turn it into the most beautiful thing you could ever dream about. He can take an unproductive life and turn it into the life of a king … but it will *not* happen overnight. Rome was not built in a day, and you will not be either. Creation did not happen in a microwave. Your re-creation will not either.

God could have wiggled His nose and produced everything He imagined in split second. If He could not have, then He's not really *God*, is He? But He intentionally did it over a sequence of time and order. He was trying to tell us (those made in His image) that we have to do it the way He did it. Change *will* happen, but it will happen step by step, day by day. Each day will establish a foundation for the next season of change. If day one does not happen, there will be no day two.

Every one of you reading these words right now is somewhere in the *yoms* of God. You are in a season of growth and change. Walk this day out, for however many hours it lasts. When this *yom* ends, there will be another to follow, but from glory to glory, God is changing you. Stay in the sequence. Keep running the race marked out for you. You're going to love what your house looks like when He's finished.

Chapter 8

The Art of Separation

Day two of creation holds quite the mystery for theologians and scientists alike. It seems there was some kind of thick water vapor surrounding the earth—so thick, in fact, that the earth and the sky could not be distinguished. The next step of God's building project was clear; there had to be a clean separation, where the earth and the sky could be seen as two separate entities. Just like in the first *yom* of creation, God spoke and this fresh work began.

In the natural, the second day of creation is not so hard to understand. God spoke, and the earth and the sky were revealed. But when we view this second day of creation through a spiritual filter, the work God is doing may not be so obvious. The key to understanding what God is doing here is found in the word "separated." It is the Hebrew word *"bandal,"* and it means to be separate, set apart, or distinguish. This word showed up on day one of creation when God separated the day from night. Now, on day two, God is at work separating more things.

Picture this in the natural. Creation begins with one big, swirling mess of gas, vapors, and debris. You can't tell what's what. It's just a big, chaotic mess. There's no form and no visible purpose for any of it. The Spirit of God begins to speak to it, though, bringing order and clarity. His work is two-fold: He begins to illuminate and then separate. He sets things apart and reveals what is day and what is night, what is earth and what is sky.

There is a word in the Bible used to encapsulate this work of illumination and separation. It's the word holiness. Holiness, or to be made holy, simply means to be separated, set apart, or distinguished. Sound familiar? It's the primary work of God's Spirit in us once we have an encounter with Him and begin to follow Him as disciples. It is a process and a command that echoes throughout Scripture, "Be holy even as I (God) am holy" (1 Peter 1:16).

It was early in the creation process that God introduced this phase of construction. It happened on day one, it's happening on day two, and by the way, it's going to continue into day three. It's an essential part of God's order that must precede future days of fruitfulness and productivity.

This work of holiness is one of the more redundant pictures laced throughout the Bible. It is represented as the Refiner's fire, the Potter's wheel, and the winepress. It is the work of God described in Hebrews 4:12 as the writer speaks of God's words being a "double-edged sword that penetrates and separates body, soul, and spirit." This same writer would go on to say in Hebrews 12:14, "Without this work of holiness, no one will see God."

Holiness is so key to God's ordered steps of construction that His covenant with Abraham and Abraham's seed were based on it. The sign of this covenant on man's end would be circumcision. Don't start feeling awkward, but I want to make sure you understand what circumcision is. It is the removal or cutting off of the foreskin of a man's reproductive organ. You need to understand that in ancient cultures, hygiene was not like today. While we may be used to taking hot showers with lots of fancy soaps every day, in Abraham's culture, men were lucky to get a cold bath in the river once a week. Because of that, most diseases a man could get that could affect his ability to reproduce would come from uncleanness associated with his foreskin.

I'm not very sure what went through Abraham's mind when God told him the sign of covenant was going to be circumcision (Gen. 17). I feel sure his first response was probably not recorded in the Bible. I'm thinking there may have been a, "Do what?" or "Could you please repeat that?" on Abe's end of the conversation. The truth is, though, Abraham may not have even remotely understood at the time why God chose circumcision to precede the many promises God made to him. He may not have seen the spiritual symbolism of cutting off flesh that could prevent him from producing fruit. When Abraham followed the practice of circumcision, God made promises to him that he would produce lots of children, and despite Abraham and Sarah's advanced age, God made good on those promises.

Abraham's story is redundant to the story of creation. Works of separation and holiness are followed by days of fruitfulness and reproduction, but even this work of separation has a very intentional order. On day two, God's only concern was to separate the earth and the sky (heavens). Under the spiritual microscope, we can begin to see God's first big step to the work of holiness He desires to do in us. It's simply to separate what is heaven and what is earth. Let me say it like this: He separates what is spiritual and what is carnal (natural). Keep in mind that we are spiritual beings having a natural experience. God needs to bring us into the illumination of what parts of us are spirit and what parts are carnal. The separation of these two realms is essential to continue deeper into God's building program for our lives.

Allow me to make this thing really practical for you. My office is a revolving door for people with problems. They can be anything from addiction, to marriage and family conflicts, to finances, to a host of emotional problems. The first order of conversation is always to allow those seeking help to speak, laying out everything in their lives that is chaotic, empty, and depressed out on the table. The second order of our conversation is that I begin to speak into their lives in an attempt to sort through the debris and figure out what is the disease and what are merely symptoms. Simply put, I try to help shed some light on the situation. It is my job to try to find a starting point to take their mess and over time, turn it into something functional, productive, and beautiful.

Now remember that I am a pastor first and a counselor second, so the third part of our conversation revolves around a spiritual line of questioning. No matter what the original problem was thought to be, I begin to probe into a person's spiritual condition. I ask about people's prayer lives, if they've been spending any time in God's Word, and if they've been in consistent fellowship at church. I am, in fact, separating their heaven and their earth.

You see, most people come into my office very aware of their symptoms, but very few know what their disease is. In fact, most think the symptoms are their disease. Let me give you an example. We are a church with great emphasis on family. Therefore, marriage ministry is a centerpiece of our church. When people come to my office for marriage counseling, they are always sure what the problem is: their spouse. But if, through my probing, I find I am dealing with people who have almost no personal devotional life and may even be sporadic in their church attendance, then suddenly the situation becomes more illuminated. If their spiritual condition is a mess, it is almost certain that whatever is manifesting in their marriage is a spiritual reflection.

If people come to me with broken finances, I must separate their heaven and earth. If they are not tithing, it will do no good to simply give them a blueprint for budgeting and investing. Their natural state is a trickle-down effect from spiritual ignorance or disobedience. If we fix the spiritual part of that person, the natural will almost always reflect new health.

One of my single biggest concerns today regarding America is how trigger-happy doctors have become when it comes to medicating people's problems. We are becoming a generation that will lose our ability to problem solve and deal with conflict if we are not careful. To be fair, there clearly are situations where medications are warranted for emotional and mental balance, but it would also be fair to say that there are many more who attempt to medicate their earth when the problem lies in their heavens. I've got news for you guys: God wired us to be emotional basket-cases if we are not in communion with Him. If our fellowship with God and with His people are suffering, it will manifest in our natural man. The apostle Paul was even bold enough in 1 Corinthians 11:30 to say that some were sick in their bodies because their fellowship with the body of Christ was sick.

Whatever our issues are today, we must allow the Holy Spirit to first illuminate the truth of what's going on, separate the spiritual from the natural, and find priority in how we address our problems. God knows that we are very prone to thinking our problems are natural when they often are spiritual. That's why my first rule of thumb when counseling is to require the person or family to get into consistent fellowship in the church for a few weeks before we actually start our sessions together. I must tell you, the percentage of people who no longer feel they need counseling after soaking in some teaching, getting in the presence of God during worship, and fellowshipping with some other believers is not-so-surprisingly high. The healing of the spirit always trickles into the mind, emotions, and often even the body of man.

God's blueprint to turn an empty life into a life of abundance requires a strict protocol. They are ordered steps that need to be followed in a specific, principled order that leads to a finished work that can only be described as a beautiful garden. For Joshua and his generation, this work of holiness—or circumcision—led into a land described as "flowing with milk and honey." It's a destination of beauty, peace, joy, abundance, fruitfulness, purpose, authority ... but you can't get there taking any old road you want. The road that dumps out in this Garden of Eden is a narrow road—a road Jesus said few would find.

So what's going on in your life? How's your marriage, your home, and your job? What's going on in your emotions and your mind? Do words like chaos, dark, depressed, or empty describe your life? Have you had an encounter with God but your life is still a wreck? There is good news! Many of you simply need to let the Spirit of God do a work of holiness in you, separating the spirit and the flesh. Some of you are exhausted from trying to fix things in the natural when the repair needs to happen in your spirit. Yield your life, will, and heart to the Lord. Ask Him to shine His light into your life, and be open to what He shows you. Pray as David did, "Search my heart, Lord, and see if there is any unclean thing in me." Allow God to come circumcise your heart, as the apostle Paul encouraged us to do. Plug back into fellowship with God through prayer while pondering His Word, and get in some good worship services. Line your spirit up with God's principles of tithing and serving the body of Christ. See if the life Jesus promised will not begin to fill your empty vessel. Separate your heavens and earth. Address the heavens, and then we'll take a second look at your earth on day three.

Chapter 9

Not Your Grandpa's Holiness

I don't really know if they would be willing to enter my accomplishment in the *Guinness Book of World Records*. To tell you the truth, I can't even guarantee I own the record, but between the ages of twelve and nineteen, I'm pretty sure I "got saved" somewhere around 2,758 times ... that being a rough guess, of course. The sequence would go something like this: I would be scared or bribed to the altar, have a good emotional breakdown with God, and go home feeling pretty good that my name was once again recorded in the Lamb's Book of Life—whatever that meant. Following my born-again (again) experience, I would have a less-than-perfect week, go back to church, hear a good ol' Pentecostal sermon on holiness, and was pretty sure I was lost again. Of course, then it was time to hit the altar again.

Now let me tell you with all sincerity in my heart that I am grateful for my Pentecostal roots. It was priceless to grow up in a church environment that taught me about the power of God and the reality of the supernatural realm. But while my mind was being renewed by the realities of God's power, it was also suffering some pretty major tissue damage from manmade holiness teachings. As I look back, the cycle I underwent is really quite funny but not in a ha-ha way. The preacher would entice us to the altar with promises of freedom if we would just give our hearts to Jesus, but those altar calls were usually preceded by a sermon on holiness that only heaped bondage on us, which is why we always felt the promise of freedom was a good reason to give our lives over to Jesus … again. You could go to church thinking you were saved, but by the time the altar call came around, you realized you were mistaken. One thing's for sure: the holiness-style preaching I grew up with may not have produced a lot of spiritual maturity in me, but it sure enough made the annual "salvation stats" at our church look pretty impressive. The only thing they didn't tell you was the five hundred people who got saved that year were the same twenty people over and over again.

Many of you reading this book can identify with the bondage, guilt, and exhaustion that come with man's idea of holiness. The stress of trying to measure up to God often becomes so overwhelming that today there are thousands of good people who are not in church simply because they were finally convinced they just couldn't do it. I am convinced that the labor-intensive-style preaching of holiness in much of the Body of Christ has destroyed more lives than any devil could ever hope for.

The irony is that Jesus really did come to set us free from this "working hard at it" style of knowing God. He said, "Come to me, all you who are weary and burdened, and I will give you rest" (Matt. 11:28). He was talking to a culture that had been buried under the weight of the Law—a people who were convinced that God would only want to connect with them from a distance because of their inability to attain His standard. "Be holy because I am holy," said God. *Right! How?* The harder we work at it, the more we fail at it.

As I see it, there have only been two primary breakdowns in the church: our presentation of grace and our presentation of holiness. When I say that, I mean it exactly in that order. There is a way to build a house with sanity and a way to do it where it will not even be functional as a place of dwelling. If I build walls with no foundation, the whole house will eventually sink. If I build walls and then try to pour a foundation on top of the walls, that's just going to make a big mess, isn't it?

The truth is that grace is *the* cornerstone of our faith. Yeah, I know, the cornerstone is Jesus—but is it Jesus the man or what He came to do? He came to establish a connection—a covenant between God and man—based on *grace*. If we don't lay that foundation correctly, there's nowhere we can take the building project from there. If God's love, grace, mercy, compassion, patience, and outright fondness for man are not *first* of all revealed to us, then everything else we attempt to teach will be misunderstood and may even do more damage than good. If we don't understand the nature of God as a *Father*, our perspective of God will be distorted, perverted, and outright misrepresented. Grace is the unmerited favor of God, and it is *impossible* for anyone to even contemplate approaching, connecting, or attaining relationship with God outside of this great grace.

There's an order to how you build a house, both natural and spiritual. There is an order to how God pours teaching and revelation into humankind to build people into spiritual dwellings where He can reside. Here's the bottom line: grace has to be the first and primary foundation established in us if we ever hope to walk with God and understand the big picture of what He's up to on planet earth. The very next step in the building project is teaching people about holiness, but if we don't understand grace, holiness will be very much misunderstood. If people don't have a decent level of revelation about God's grace for the believer, holiness teaching will destroy much more than it builds up. If our minds are not renewed to the loving favor of our God, holiness teaching will not set people free. It will, in fact, put them in deeper bondage than they were in before giving their lives to Christ. Hebrews 12:14 says, "Without holiness no one will see the Lord," but if that holiness is not presented in the right way and the right order, it will guarantee that man will *never* see God.

The book of Genesis tells about the origin of man and the world he lives in. It's the story of how God made it all and made it to function productively. It's the story of a natural earth and what was made from the dust of the earth (us). It's the story of chaos having an encounter with God and the transformation that can take place because of it. It's an architectural blueprint of order that, when followed step by step, allows for such an incredible transformation.

Chaos has an encounter with the Spirit of God—the Father of Creation. There is illumination or revelation that quickly ensues. But even within the first *yom* of man's encounter with God, works of separation (holiness) began. On day one, day and night were separated. On day two, the heavens and the earth were separated. Now, it's day three, and guess what? That's right, more separation. God begins a new season of speaking into the earth and commands the waters to be separated from the land.

I want you to see this funnel approach to God's stages of holiness. On day two, He separates the heavens from the earth so we can see what part of our condition is spiritual and what part is natural. On day three, He is focused just on the earth or the natural. The spiritual realties have been identified, and now the finer points of holiness are being addressed in our carnal earth.

The great teacher of new-covenant holiness was the apostle Paul. He was also the great instructor on grace, by the way. Paul was very detailed in passages like Romans 8 when it came to separating the spiritual side of man from the carnal. With great passion, he dealt with this day–two type of holiness. He also dealt with a lot of day-three-type holiness. He would send letters to church after church outlining areas of their lifestyle that were counterproductive to the call of God in their lives. He would speak to them about issues such as gossip, envy, slander, jealousy, and self-centeredness. The list of sins in our carnal nature that Paul addressed is actually way too lengthy to document in this book, but when you read Paul's writings, they are commonly spoken about. These are issues in man's earth—his carnal nature—that Paul pressed the people to deal with.

I want to be clear here. Despite how man has presented holiness teaching, the issues of the flesh Paul addressed were not what we would call heaven and hell issues. In other words, these issues of the flesh were things I was sure I was going to swim in flames for eternity over, but Paul was writing to the church, the sons and daughters of God—those in *grace* covenant with God. These were not issues that affected God's love or acceptance of them. *Nothing can separate us from the love of god*, Paul proclaims in Romans 8. However, what these deeds of the carnal nature *can* do is separate us from the abundant life Jesus promised us.

Here's where things have been a little misleading in Christian theology. It is true that the promises of God are a pretty convincing sales pitch for many, if not most, who currently are disciples of Jesus Christ. Jesus said He came to bring us life and that life would be abundant. Sign me up. To know God is to know peace. Hey, I'm all about that. His joy is unspeakable and full of glory. Yeah, I want some of that, too. A life of fruitfulness, purpose, and destiny? Of course, count me in. I want this stuff, and according to what I've always heard preached, it's supposed to be mine. So how come so many believers are clearly not walking in any of the aforementioned promises?

People go to church and do all the churchy stuff, but where is all this life Jesus talked about? We've responded to every altar call, traveled hundreds of miles to hear the hottest conference speakers, read their books, gave extra offerings, increased our devotion time, went to six weeks of counseling, and had our meds increased ... *what are we missing!*

I'm glad you asked! If we go back to the original blueprint that was drawn by the Architect of humanity, we see the missing link: *holiness!* This incredible work of God's Spirit clearly precedes the seasons of fruitfulness that later show up in the creation process. In fact, before the third *yom* of God was over in this beautiful story, fruit was being produced, *but* only after seasons of holiness were orchestrated in the earth.

This essential work of God is proclaimed throughout the Bible with great redundancy. In the Old Testament, this work of holiness was often referred to as consecration. In the New Testament, it is often called sanctification. Both are words that mean to be made holy, set apart, or distinguished. Great promises of God were always linked to actions of consecration and sanctification. Great victories and prosperity were realized following seasons of holiness.

Jesus' greatest conversation on holiness is found in John 15. He speaks of Himself as the vine, us as the branches, and the Father as the gardener. He presents in great detail the model of the gardener cutting off branches in our lives that keep us from producing fruit. Jesus said, "This is to my Father's glory, that you produce MUCH fruit, showing yourselves to be my disciples" (vs. 8). This was a promise of *much* fruit … following the pruning of unfruitful branches.

It is these unfruitful branches that Paul addresses in his many letters to the church. They are things of the flesh, as we call them, that prevent us from stepping into the things God promised us. But it is imperative that we don't see these works of holiness through the filter of Law. Perceiving the holiness works of God with a legalistic mind will only further separate you from God's promises. What was meant to make you fruitful will only land you in jail.

We must understand that being holy as God is holy is absolutely a choice. It is a work of the Spirit that we must agree with because God will not force you to be pruned. But we must also understand that if we *give* our lives to God, He has the right to introduce us to these ordered steps that are designed to make our lives full. If we run from holiness, we are running from God's promises. If we think there is a shortcut, we will be left short on what we think God has promised us. If we have not stepped into a grace revelation first, we will misunderstand holiness to be further bondage of the law. If we sidestep the holiness works of God's order, we will be left confused, wondering why God's Word doesn't work for us.

We have avoided and dismissed the essentials of God for far too long in the body of Christ. We must allow God to illuminate His grace and love for us so we can get on with the process of holiness. We must get settled in who we are to the Father so we can give Him permission to put us on the Potter's wheel without us battling condemnation. We need to be agreeable to the refiner's fire that purges us of impurities so we can become pure gold. We need to become excited that God is swinging His double-edged sword in our lives, separating spirit and flesh. We need to be optimistic about the sweet wine that will flow from our lives if we allow God to put us in the winepress. The threshing floor needs to be something that we invite into our lives, not run from.

Yeah, I know. The Refiner's fire is hot, the Potter's wheel spins you around, and in the winepress, you get stomped on—but the end result is why we all got into this race. We want our lives to be represented by fine gold, a beautiful vessel, and the most excellent of wines. That is truly what your Father, your Creator, has planned for your lives. You don't even have to waste your prayer life on begging for it. Remember, it was *His* idea. Fruitfulness and living a productive life are your destiny, your birthright. There is a path that leads you there. There are steps that will take you in that direction. There is a blueprint that absolutely calls for that kind of life for you. So get your ducks in a row. Jump into God's process of holiness with both feet. Sure, it'll burn a little. That's the point, right?

Chapter 10

❧◈❧

Third-Day Life

There's something special about the third day in Scripture. It was on the third day that Jesus rose from the grave. Out of the ashes of death, life sprang up. It is also on the third day of creation that we first see life springing up. Finally, after multiple works of separation, the work of the Spirit is beginning to produce life in what once was a dark, desolate wasteland. God speaks, and vegetation begins to exist—and not just vegetation for the purpose of greening the place up a little; these were plants and trees that produced seed and fruit.

It's also very important to notice the perpetual fruit-producing potential this life of day three actually held. God commanded the plant life to produce seed and fruit that would produce seed and fruit. In other words, God was putting a harvest in motion within the very first season of life showing up. Day three was not just an impartation of life for the moment but the resurrection of life that would begin an endless journey of continual increase.

Producing fruit and harvest are by far some of the more recurring themes of the Bible. Within the redundant framework of these topics, God's concern for us doing more with our lives than simply existing in the moment is clear. John the Baptist summed it up best when he said, "Produce fruit in keeping with your repentance"

(Matt. 3:8). A modern-day translation of this unconventional prophet would be this: "Don't just get saved and go to church. Do something productive with your life." This ragtag desert preacher's message preceded the message of the one greater than himself. "You did not choose me, but I chose you and appointed you to go and bear fruit—fruit that will last." Jesus made clear in these words we pull from John 15 that we are saved for a purpose: to have a fruitful life. The apostle Paul echoes the heart of God and even clarifies to multiple churches that it is, in fact, our fruitfulness that the Lord finds very pleasing in our lives.

As a dad, I am completely on board with this desire God has for His children. In fact, there is not a day that goes by that I don't in some way attempt to inspire or motivate my daughter to learn and excel in life. I am constantly offering her incentives and rewards in every area of life that is preparing her for her future. Seeing her tap into her potential in school, dance, music, and all the other creative areas of her life is at the top of my pleasure-chart. When she brings home an A on a reading test, she usually gets a little extra favor. When she pushes through her insecurities and dances on the big stage in front of a crowd of people, she gets something special next time we go to Wallyworld (that's Wal-Mart to those of you living in caves). Every area of her life where she is currently producing fruit is preparing her to produce even more fruit later on in life. As her dad, watching this progression exhilarates me. Not only does it bring me great personal joy, but it also motivates me to equip her with whatever she needs in each stage of her life.

God has been abundantly—if not redundantly—clear about His plan for us to be fruitful in life. We don't have to beg Him for it or attempt some backdoor plan to gain His favor for fruitfulness. *It was His idea.* You don't have to measure up, but you will have to go through some process of separation. The bottom line, though, is that God really, really, really wants you to have a full, productive, fruitful life. You know—the opposite of how you were when you first came to Him empty and useless. Your Daddy wants you to excel in life, be all you can be, and find great purpose in your existence. He has put a gift in you that, when extracted and used, can produce a great harvest in your life and in the lives of those around you.

From the midpoint of day three of creation until the completion of day six, we see a clear progression of life. A season that begins with vegetation leads to a new season where life shows up in even fuller ways. God speaks, and the air is filled with birds and the waters are filled with fish. That season leads to yet another season of life where animals begin to fill the earth, and by the end of the day, humankind itself is created. From "glory to glory," God progressively, step by step, took life from the most basic form to the most complex. It's a picture of harvest—the increase of God's kingdom in humanity. With each newly ordered day came a newer, deeper, richer level of life. With each *yom* of fruitfulness came a new *yom* where spiritual maturity and its rewards were realized.

This picture of creation, while also very literal, is a spiritual schematic to God's perfect will for mankind. It is the answer to what Jesus prayed when He said, "Thy Kingdom come, Thy will be done." This prayer that is the model for how we all should pray was a cry for God's order to be reestablished in us. It was a petition to rediscover the original blueprint God had for turning an empty life into a productive one. It is a level of God's will that supersedes the more elementary pursuit of church position. It *is* His will and order from which all life flows.

Psalm 139 says that in your mother's womb, God knew you and very carefully and meticulously knit your natural body parts together. While this passage first speaks of the natural, it then turns to the spiritual: "All the *days* ordained for me were written in your book before one of them came to be" (v. 16). These are not the days of being a doctor, lawyer, or Indian chief. These recorded days are the *yoms* of God, the ordered steps that take your life from being undistinguished and formless in the womb of life to a fully formed, functional man or woman of fruitfulness.

God has called you to a life of holiness. It is His will and His ordered steps for your life. The purpose of it all is that you might be fruitful, which is *also* His perfect will for your life.

Chapter 11

The Day of the Lord

As I grow older, I look back with more and more fondness on that season of my life when God began to radically transform me. My life truly was represented by that early picture we see in the creation story. Chaos, emptiness, lack of purpose, and darkness accurately described my condition. It really is amazing to me now how quickly things changed as I began to have an encounter with God and allowed Him to speak into my world. He pulled me deep into His arms of love and coated me with grace that became so much bigger than my many sins. My acceptance of His love helped me to also accept the works of holiness He ushered me into. It was my first stage of walking with God as we partnered to bring multiple levels of separation into my life. With each new season of holiness came new seasons of life. An existence that was previously marred with an empty hope of a better someday was, in fact, beginning to produce some pretty amazing fruit. Life was truly beginning to show up on my planet.

God is changing us from glory to glory, though. As long as we stay in that process of change, we're bound to enter into a new season of God that raises the bar considerably higher than any prior season of growth. That season for me, and I believe for all who have had a genuine encounter with God, is very well represented in day four of creation.

Genesis1:14–19 proclaims day four to be the *yom* when the sun, moon, and stars were hung in the heavens. To be very honest, it really would appear in the natural that this God of great, methodical order I've been talking about got things a little bit out of sequence here. The invention of the sun should not follow the creation of plant life; it should be just the opposite. This is not good government. Maybe someone mixed up the pages of the blueprint and stapled them back together out of order. But wait! What if there happens to be great method to God's apparent sequential madness? We know the Bible is clear that "God's ways are not the ways of man." Maybe that's the message God is sending here—that His ways will seem foolish to the carnal mind. But even though I will be the first to agree that God's ways sometimes seem out of order for us—even downright crazy at times—we are not looking at this creation story through a natural filter but a spiritual one. In God's realm, which is a spiritual realm, His order *always* makes perfect sense. Every sequence of change is incredibly methodical and intentional.

As I matured spiritually, God's progressive staircase of change took me into a day-four experience where new demands were made on my life that challenged all the preexisting days of creation. It took me into a season that no longer seemed to be all about me and the wonderful new life God was building for me. It was a season that radically altered my view of God, the position He had been holding in my life, and the new position He wanted to hold.

The Bible says that on day four of creation, God hung the sun, moon, and stars in the heavens. While Genesis calls both of these lights "great," the sun would be referred to as the "greater" of the two. These lights had a very specific purpose; they were to *govern*. The sun would govern the day, and the moon would govern the night.

Naturally speaking, none of us has to be a great scientist to understand the literal day four. Viewing this day through a spiritual filter is actually almost just as easy. Let's apply the most basic of hermeneutical skills here. By the way, hermeneutics is simply the theological science of Bible interpretation. The most fundamental and basic tool any sound theologian would use to ascertain the context of abstract biblical passages is this: *it is always best to interpret Scripture using Scripture.* When we do that and keep human imagination out of the mix, the Bible is not really so hard to understand. The dots connect easier than you may think, and the folly of God suddenly can make a lot of sense to the mind that has been renewed by the washing of the Word.

With that being said, we can overlay later Scripture onto day four of creation and safely define the imagery God uses. The sun is the greater light—God Himself—and the moon its reflection in the earth—Jesus Christ. My favorite passage using this imagery is Joel's prophecy that Peter echoes in Acts 2:20: "The sun will be turned to darkness and the moon to blood before the coming of the great and glorious Day of the Lord." Oh how that abstract prophetic picture comes to life on Calvary's hill as the Father turns His face away from His sin-encrusted Son as He drips His life blood onto the earth. That day the earth manifested the events of heaven as the earth was covered with darkness.

Simply seeing the abstract imagery of the Father and the Son in day four holds little insight to the progressive order of God's blueprint of change though. The key is found within the *purpose* of these great lights. They were to *govern*, rule, and call the shots. Day four is a day of lordship when all that has been saved in our lives must now be yielded to the one who saved them to fulfill *His* plans and purposes. It's a season when we make intentional decisions to submit to the rule of God, giving Him all rights and ownership privileges. It's a *yom* during which we begin to walk in the personal revelation that *everything* was created by Him and *for* Him.

One of my clearer observations of the body of Christ is that day four of the blueprint is the primary place where a breakdown happens in many people's construction project. Most people are thrilled when God steps into their lives and begins to turn their chaos into something beautiful. Oh, the jubilation I have witnessed as God begins to produce fruit out of people's emptiness. The joy of new life is unspeakable and full of glory when we finally find purpose. God has done so much for us, but at some point, the honeymoon days lead to a season where we begin to sense God is making demands that at first grate against our flesh. We love what He has done with our lives, but we wonder why He has to mess it all up by wanting to come in and *govern* us. Couldn't He be happy just being our Savior, our Santa Claus, our Mr. Fix-It? But *nooo*, He wants to be the boss of me. He wants to be my *Looord*. (By the way, make sure that you read those last couple of sentences with childish sarcasm in your voice.)

Day four is where the journey gets bogged down for humanity at large. We saw it in Abraham's father, Terah. He started for Canaan—the land flowing with milk and honey—but settled halfway in a place called Haran and died there. Haran, by the way, means dry or parched. Later those in Moses' generation did the same thing. They were set free from the dark bondage of Egypt and began a progressive journey to Canaan—you know, the milk and honey place. But they also failed to move past the midpoint of the journey and died in a dry, parched wilderness. God had something better for them than *just* being saved. His plans were bigger than just eating the manna and quail that were on the wilderness menu. God promised them a land where the fruit was so big they would barely be able to carry it, but they settled for early days of salvation and separation from Egypt. Though God had distinguished them as the children of the living God, they died without seeing the full blueprint of God for their lives realized.

Days one, two, and three of creation hold the tale of salvation and wonderful works of holiness that distinguish us as blessed children of the living God. They are days when life and fruit begin to show up. But the life and fruit of the first three days are nothing compared to the level of life we see later in the last three days of construction. The river that divides these two realms of fruitfulness is day four. It's a season where Jesus becomes *Lord* of our lives—a day when He rules and calls the shots and when our lives are no longer about us but about Him. I am sad that so many never cross into this season of God and actually partake of God's richest promises.

I want to be clear that making Jesus Lord of our lives is not found within our "lordship" terminology. Singing, "He is Lord" does not, in fact, make Him our Lord. Jesus said in Matthew 7:21, "Not everyone who says to me Lord, Lord, will enter the Kingdom of Heaven." He went on to say in Luke 6:46, "Why do you call me Lord, and do not do what I say?" You see, His lordship requires our obedience, surrender, and transfer of ownership of our lives to Him. Lordship is found within the tangible relinquishing of our wills, skills, and purpose. It is a dying to ourselves—a crucifixion of our flesh.

Jesus said, "If you want to have life, you must give your life away." He's speaking of allowing Him to be Lord of our lives. His lordship is a key to the very Kingdom of Heaven, a place of the now where righteousness, peace, and joy are the fruit of its forests (Rom. 14:17). Throughout the Bible, this realm of life is depicted as almost-utopian in its gains, favor, and position. It is a promised reality Jesus called, "Life and life abundant." *But* these seasons only follow a day-four stage of construction. If this page of the blueprint is skipped, you might as well throw away the pages that follow. The land flowing with milk and honey is for a Joshua generation that—unlike the Moses generation—yielded their lives in obedience to God's lordship. One generation was content with being "saved" and existing off of life-maintenance miracles while the other inherited great victories, the spoils of great cities, and the fruit of great prosperity.

I know all of this lordship stuff can sound pretty sacrificial on the surface, but I can tell you from firsthand experience that giving up your rights of ownership is not as bad as it sounds. Sure, up front it was a little bit of a shock to find out that God's blueprint for my life was really about building Him a house, but as His lordship grew in my life, my understanding was matured. Then I began to realize the life He was building in me was not *just* for Him; it was for both of us to enjoy together. If it were not for His lordship in my life, I would have lived in a very selfish way, using all the wonderful things He was doing in me just for myself. Allowing Him to be the Lord of my life (which is still a work in progress, by the way) has taught me how to find purpose I would have never found if I had ruled my own life. The Savior who then became my Lord has directed my steps down paths of destiny that have blown away my early days of salvation.

I want to show you another perk found in a day-four season of lordship that has provided me with a level of peace beyond description. Genesis 1:14 says these governing lights are to "serve as signs and mark the seasons." We all understand the natural context of that statement. The distance of the sun from the earth helps to differentiate the four major seasons, and the fullness of the moon helps us determine the time of the month. The combination of the two can mark major holidays. In other words, these great governing lights are the signs to tell you where you are on the calendar at different times of the year. Spiritually, it all speaks of knowing where you are in God's will at different seasons of life. Very plainly put, because of His lordship in our lives, we are not so confused about what the moon (no pun intended) is going on in our lives. I see confused Christians all the time who are experiencing the conflicts of life that stress them out as they try and determine if it's God or the devil opposing them. They are confused about every little thing that happens in life, wondering if it's a sign from God and what it all really means, and they are anxious as they labor to "seek God's will for their life." My friends, this should not be.

As much as my initial encounter with God meant in my life, with all the life-inducing changes that came with it in those early days, allowing His lordship has taken me into even deeper levels of life. It has brought back a security and confidence that keeps me tracking forward and not looking back. While others have stayed bogged down for years in a struggle to ascertain "God's will for their lives," I have been free to advance into destiny. His lordship in my life has produced a peace in the midst of my storms that never has me second guessing Him or the fact that I know my ship is still on course. If my journey does get off kilter a little, it is quickly corrected without drama, sweat, or tears.

Jesus did not save us just so we can go to heaven and not have to go to hell. If we remain in that "saved from" mentality, we will die in confusion, wondering why we never saw the things God promised. We will only be those who observe the promises of God from a distance as we hear the testimonies of those who did cross over into the Promised Land. We must get a "saved for" mindset. We are saved *for* the rights to rule, reign, produce great fruit, find the promise of purpose and destiny, and inherit abundant life—*right here, right now!* It *is* through making Jesus your *Lord* that this is realized.

Some of you need to stop wrestling with God, the devil, and yourselves and simply enter an intentional season of learning and experience the Lordship of God. Trust me, there is a comfort to Him owning your life that sweetens the deal considerably. I know—our flesh hates the concept of someone else telling us what to do. But if that someone happens to be the Creator of the universe who loved us so much He died for us, how bad can it be?

Jesus said it all in His short parable found in Luke 6:46–49. In fact, that parable is the total synopsis of creation's day four. He compares a man who builds his house on solid foundation to a man who builds his house with no foundation at all. When the storms came, one house stood and one house fell. The secret to the house that stood was found upon the deed of ownership. It was the house that had made Jesus Lord of the castle.

Where are you at in the ordered steps of God? Is there any chance this is the page of the blueprint God has turned to in your life? If it is, I encourage you to learn to submit with joy. Fighting His lordship is fighting against your own future. Let today be the season your knees bow and your tongue confess, *"He is lord!"* You're gonna love the level of life that follows.

Chapter 12

The Man in the Mirror

I suspect the average human mind does not have the ability to appreciate the climax of creation's day six. From day three, we watch as God becomes progressively more intense in the complex nature of His handiwork. He progresses from plants to birds and fish to land animals to … *humans*. With each natural day, the natural function of everything, from the ecosystems to the biological systems of a living, breathing creature, is more than enough to prove a methodical higher power had to be involved. For me, it would take considerably more faith to believe the end product of creation haphazardly evolved from a cosmic explosion than by the intentional design of a divine being of order. You see, there just aren't any good secular explanations that hold water scientifically. While I am not a scientist, I am also not a complete novice. I have carefully studied most secular theories that currently exist and find they always end up leading to a dead end where important questions cannot be answered. In other words, no matter what the theory is, there are huge gaps that are based on presumption, assumption, and unproven ideologies. There is no proof that simple cells can become complex cells, which destroys the theory of evolution. In other words, the cells that make up a mud puddle are not capable of evolving into a complex state of supporting intelligence. It is *all* based on a lot of theory and a lot of denial.

The creation account of the Bible leaves no gaps in the function of life, though. Genesis says that God created all the plants and animals to reproduce after their own kind. That's not to say that one dog can't be educated to be smarter than another dog. It also doesn't mean that God didn't wire into life's systems the ability to adapt to different environments if exposed to them long enough. However, those types of alterations are not a change in the primary DNA structure of those creatures. No, my friends, the perfect operating order of life and all of its compatible systems scream for an explanation more logical than mud pies and walking catfish.

My role, however, is not to be another author attempting to convince you of the truth of the Genesis account of creation. There are plenty of authors out there who have done a much better job of that than I could do. This book is really written to those who already believe God created the universe but who may not truly understand the whole story of what happened on the evening of day six. Yes, a little research tells us that God's last action of creation on day six was the creation of humankind. The part of day six that I believe still remains a mystery to too many is just *who* the man God created actually was.

In Genesis 1:26, God said, "Let us make man in our image, in our likeness, and let them rule ..." This word "image" is the Hebrew word *tselem,* which, like most Hebrew words, holds a plethora of possible substitute terms. The word image was the word selected by Bible translators long ago, but it may not be the most user-friendly term in our culture. But *tselem* also means "reflection," which is a very relatable word for us. The bottom line is this: God wanted us to know that we were a mirror reflection of who He is. Do you know how to appreciate God's first introduction of us? I'm not sure I do. The fact is, most humans (even the ones who can quote Genesis 1:26

with the best of them) put very little significant thought into to this first description of mankind.

Now that I think about it, most of us who grew up in church probably thought about this made in the image of God thing more as kids than we have as adults. As children, we used to sit around and talk about what God actually looked like. Whether George Burns or Morgan Freeman fits your imagination the best, the one thing we were sure of was that God had arms, legs, eyes, a mouth, and so on. In other words, God looked just like us … only invisible. Our theory was based on the fact that we were made in His image. Therefore, we reasoned, if we look like Him, He must look like us.

The truth is, of course, we don't know how to properly ponder a spiritual world. Unless we give tangible, physical attributes to a spirit, we cannot relate to it. Does God, who is a spirit, have eyeballs, hands, and a mouth? Well, the Bible sure talks about God seeing, touching, and talking. But does that necessarily mean He has our body parts but is just invisible? Or does it simply mean that the physical world we live in requires tangible body parts to accomplish what God does by nature in His world? Well, while we may debate that one until the end of time, I think it's safe to say that these physical features are not what God was talking about when He said we were a mirror reflection of who He is.

When God said we were made in His image, He was saying we were just like Him. The thing that goes mostly unnoticed is that God had just spent six days of creation introducing and describing Himself before he let us know we were a chip off the old block. Like Father, like Son. What is the Son supposed to be like? Easy—what was the Father like? From the start of creation when Genesis 1:1 says, "In the beginning God …," the Bible begins to describe God's personality, style, and mannerisms. After six *yoms* of activity, God has told us everything we need to know about Him so we would know everything we needed to know about us.

Meanwhile, humanity desperately searches to discover who they are and why they are here. We go on seminars, retreats, and sabbaticals and spend endless years at the feet of counselors in pursuit of identity. We go to church, focusing on how to make our lives better so we can be content and at peace with life. But it's not working. We have become professional Christians, but we're still empty and confused. *What are we missing?*

The answer will come off as simplistic and trite if it is only heard on the surface. Our problem is that we don't know God. Because we don't know who He is, we don't know who we are. Listen to this carefully, because we're overlooking what should be the obvious to the Body of Christ. When I say we don't know God, I'm not talking about sinner's prayers, having your name on the church roll, and teaching Sunday school. I'm not even talking about having a strong prayer life, religiously reading the Bible, and never missing a church service. What I'm saying is *we don't know who God is.* We don't know *who* God is because we don't know *how* God is.

It's quite funny really, but not in the proverbial ha-ha way. Most of our twentieth-century American church services were devoted to saving man, fixing his problems, and making him happier. To tell you the truth, that sounds pretty much like every religion out there. We've preached heaven, hell, the devil, and man's sin until we're blue in the face. We're well versed on all kinds of special doctrines, from prosperity to inner healing. We can describe the landscape of heaven and paint horrendous pictures of hell, way beyond what the Bible in context talks about. I've heard hour-long sermons on Satan using descriptions that I can't find in the Bible. I could go on and on. My point is, why are we not spending more time talking about *who God is?*

No wonder we're so lost … even though we're saved. No wonder we're so caught up in being caught up instead of exploring the wonders of who God made us to be. God made it all and said, "It's good!" All I heard growing up was how bad it all is and how God needed to get us out of here. Our loss of identity has perverted our mindsets, and our perverted mindsets have drawn gross conclusions as to who God is, how God is, and what this whole thing is about. We are lost, and that's why Jesus "came to save *that* which was lost" (Luke 19:10). What was lost was humanity's soul. What we forget was that in Hebrew culture, the soul contained the mind and thoughts of man. King Solomon declared, "As a man thinks, so he is" (Prov. 23:7). Man thinks he is somebody he is not; therefore, he lives beneath the way he was created. Man does not know who he is because he does not know who God is. How can we reflect what we're ignorant to? That is why our minds must be renewed or returned back to the original state in which God made us.

We have been in a theological crisis in the American church. Theology is the study of God, and we've been studying everything but Him—but times are a-changing. The Spirit of God is calling us to return to Him. The words of the prophet are coming to pass: "The earth is being filled with the *knowledge of God* like the waters fill up the sea" (Hab. 2:14).

To know God is to know who He is and how He is. Knowing who He is means I know who I am. When I know that, I can strive to be that … and it is good!

Chapter 13

Generation Regeneration

If I heard it once, I heard it a thousand times growing up: "You've got your daddy's eyes." At three years of age, my literal way of thinking confused me just a little when I heard this statement. By seven, I was starting to understand. Through the years, not just my eyes but also many personality traits would be credited to my father. Most of the time, when I was accused of acting just like my dad, it was a good thing (sometimes, however, not so much). But the bottom line was while some of my traits were acquired through learned behavior, many of my attributes were passed on to me through my dad's DNA. Our DNA is, of course, the genetic code that determines our physical appearance and much of our emotional and mental makeup. This natural process is one of many processes God built into the systems of life to help us understand how His spiritual processes work. The apostle Paul knew this understanding would be imperative for us to understand our destiny and purpose. God always uses natural terms, positions, relationships, and processes to educate us on the realities of His world. He constantly and consistently plays off of imagery we can relate to in our world so we can relate to Him in His world.

The genetics of Genesis was no doubt meant to be foundational to man's knowledge of God and of himself. Out of the dust of the earth, God formed the physical parts of man, and then from a blast of His nostrils, God deposited a genetic code in man that would guarantee legitimate offspring. This man, Adam, was supposed to be just like God in his nature and qualities. He was supposed to stand in a position of dominion and rule, just like his Father. He would, in fact, become part of the creation process with his Father, finishing the work of creation by naming the animals his Father had made. Adam's reign would be a microcosm of God's universal territories, but the child's realm of responsibility is always smaller than the parent's—right?

Creation, no doubt, began to observe this son as he learned to walk out his position as the guardian of Eden. But deceit, a fall, and failure to assume responsibility resulted in Adam losing not just his home and his position but his mind also. The trickery of the serpent pulled the psych job of the ages, and Adam forgot who he was. When Adam lost his original identity as one made in the very image of God, he also lost all God commissioned him to do and be. He was not reigning as a prince; he was laboring as a son without a home, wallowing in the pig pen of life. He became the original prodigal son. He had no power, no purpose, and no relationship with the Father he used to walk with in the cool of the day. He was lost because his identity was lost. He was dead because his connection to the Spirit that blew the very breath of life in him was severed.

Four thousand years later, God sent Jesus—whom the Bible calls the second Adam—to save and restore what the first Adam lost. A work that began on Calvary's hill initiated a rescue mission that would redeem man and restore him back to his original place in creation. Through the work of the cross, God ignited a salvation process that would begin with the reunification of the Father and His sons and end with the sons reclaiming their identity as the princes of creation. These prodigal sons could now return to their Father's house—not as slaves but as kings wearing their father's robe and signet ring. The robe of righteousness (position) and signet ring (authority) would be

placed back upon the son (humanity) by the Father Himself. And then—well, *it's party time. It's party time. Put your hands in the air like you just don't care. It's party time.*

Sorry, I got carried away there for a moment. The point is, Jesus paints a beautiful picture in the parable of the prodigal son of the great life the son experienced after coming back into his Father's house. As a result of Jesus' work on the cross, abundant, fruitful life has been returned back to mankind like he hasn't seen since walking in the garden of God. That which was lost—relationship with God and their position as kings—has been offered back to all the Adams of this world.

Buuuuuut! I know, it seems like there's always a big "but" attached to most of the good stuff. Well the but is this: as real and finished as the work of Jesus is in this process, it doesn't manifest in our everyday lives until we start thinking like the redeemed princes we are. The spiritual realities are one thing, but if we're going to realize the promises of God as more than empty, abstract illusions in the tangible world we live in, we're going to have to get back the mindset the first Adam lost. Jesus did it. Before He died to redeem us, He became the perfect pattern of how the first Adam was supposed to do it and how we will now have to do it. He took His position of dominion and earned the title of King of kings. He ruled it all—seen and unseen.

The scene fades. Jesus exits stage up. Who should enter stage right under a bright spotlight but the soon-to-be-apostle Paul. His life followed the saving work of Jesus with instructions about what now had to happen. In letter after letter, he dealt with issues that mostly fall under three headings: grace, holiness, and *godliness*. The grace and holiness parts we've already dealt with. The other great directive Paul dealt with is summed up in a word that requires very little research. The word godliness simply means to be like God. You know, to act like we are made in His likeness.

Paul doesn't just use this word. He also uses other terms and phraseologies that, in context, all refer to the same work. He talks

about being imitators of God and consistently exhorts the churches to have their minds renewed. Renewed? Yeah, you know, returned back to the original. Paul links so many of the precious commodities we seek after to this renewed state of mind. He links joy, freedom, and enjoying a great life to becoming godly (again, like God). But the greatest thing Paul ever linked to this restored or renewed mind was an understanding of God's perfect will or plan for our lives (Rom. 12:2). Paul, in fact, relegated our whole transformation process to having a restored mind.

For the past two thousand years, the plan has been simple ... well, kind of. The blood of Jesus has washed away our sin and failure, returning us to a state of peace with God. The Bible says we are now righteous before God, which simply means we are back in the original place of relationship with God. This means we are back in our original place of relationship with God as Father and sons. But despite what the half-gospel we've presented in the twentieth-century American church might say, the work of Christ is not completed in just our being saved so we can go to heaven someday. The work of God, from God's perspective, is not complete until we are restored back to seeing, believing, and living like sons of the Creator of the universe. We must reclaim the mind the first Adam lost but the second Adam redeemed for us. Our journey with God, after we have accepted the work of the cross in a personal way, is to reclaim the birthright we so easily traded for a bowl of soup in the Garden of Eden six thousand years ago. Our identity is no longer found in Esau, a wandering man who was only concerned with survival and temporal maintenance. We are Jacob, a spiritual Israel whose identity is known as Abraham's seed, the highly favored children of God. We are the head and not the tail. We are kings, priests, and a chip off the cornerstone of God.

We live in exciting times where the truths of who God is (and who we are) are beginning to be rediscovered. We are finding our identity as those who live in a Most Holy Place, the very castle of

God. We are remembering we were born to rule and reign in a kingdom that not only belongs to the Father but His sons also. It's coming back to us now that we are joint heirs with the King of kings, which is a mind-blowing *now* statement that is beyond our mental ability to process.

We are being regenerated, re-gened with the DNA (Divine Nature Acquired) of the eternal God of the universe. It's a season in church history I like to call Generation Regeneration. I've got good news for you: this process of regeneration (taking on the nature of God) is not as complex as the church sometimes makes it out to be. It's simply seeing how God is and then intentionally imitating Him. The more we imitate Him, the more His nature begins to invade our nature. At some point, if we mimic Him long enough, that original nature we were created with will resurrect from the grave and become our new life.

Now let me remain clear before we move on: godliness or to be godly, means being like God. I grew up in churches where godliness was taught as a long list of things we should refrain from. If I didn't drink, cuss, or fornicate, I was being godly, since He didn't do those things. But godliness is not about the labor of abstaining or refraining from things. That "church lifestyle" is merely a legalistic return to the Tree of Knowledge of Good and Evil. No, pursuing godliness is a joyful journey of observing God's nature from His Word and intentionally adapting to those same attributes. We see how God thinks (and acts), and we follow His lead. Like father, like son. His DNA runs through our spiritual veins, and our purpose in life is to become just like Him.

Chapter 14

A Portrait of God

The call of God upon humanity is pretty well laid out through the pages of the Bible. It is a call for relationship. Everything God tells us to do and not do becomes part of the means to that end. But being in relationship with God, or anyone else, for that matter, begins with knowing about Him. By that I mean knowing the parts of God that are actually relatable. I can't relate to God as having always existed. That's beyond my ability to process. To be honest with you, I really can't relate to God as the Creator of the universe either. Maybe you've done some things on the level of the spectacular and can relate to the fathomless details of God's handiwork. I cannot. I believe He did it, but believing it and relating to it are two completely different things.

What I can relate to, though, is God's nature. Any type of personality trait, emotion, method, or motivation God and I share makes God relatable to me. The more I get to know how God is, the more I understand who God is. The more I begin to know who God is through learning about His nature, the more He and I are in true relationship. This conformity to His nature is the work of godliness, which we have been talking about in the two previous chapters. This call of godliness is essential to the overall plan of God for our lives.

The promises of God's Word for our life, power for living, and life abundant all hinge on where we are in this process. It defines who we are and where we are going in life.

So let me say it like this: our identity as one made in God's image is 100 percent reliant upon knowing who God is first. We will never know who we are if we don't open our eyes up to see just who He is. We cannot reflect what we cannot see.

The Architect of Eden very intentionally designed us after a perfect pattern: Himself. When God sent His Son, Jesus, it was to remind us of the pattern. Jesus said, "If you've seen me, you've seen the Father." By the way, anyone who calls him or herself a son of God who stays in the process of holiness and godliness long enough should be able to say the same thing with great confidence. We're not saying we're perfect, as man would think. We are simply saying our mind, emotions, and actions are just like our Daddy's.

On day six of creation, God invented man. What do we know about this man? Well, we know God formed his natural parts from the dust of the earth and blew the breath of life into him, and he became a living creature. But that doesn't tell us anything about *who* he is and *how* he is supposed to operate. God made him and told him to rule over creation and walk in a place of dominion in the earth. But where's the explanation for how this was supposed to happen?

The simple truth though is that God spent all six days of creation telling man everything he would ever need to know about himself. God said He made humans in His image, so all we have to do is go back and see everything God showed us about Himself to see the reflection. For six *yoms,* God introduced Himself, created us, and said, "Oh, by the way, you're just like Me."

I realize the Bible is packed full of stories, commands, and principles—and it's *all* really good stuff. *But* most of what you need to know about who God is—and therefore who you are—is pretty much portrayed in the creation story of Genesis and repeated in the life of Jesus. Sure, there's always frosting, candles, and a few frills we can add to the top of the cake, but God clearly laid the foundation of His nature for us in the very beginning. If we want to know what God's reflection (humanity) is supposed to look like, we must look at the original pattern. The prophet Ezekiel said, "Show the house to the house." In other words, if you look at God, then you'll know who you are. Your nature is His nature. How He did it is how you'll have to do it. How He felt is how you should feel.

Have you been on a journey searching to know who you are? Well, you will never know who you are until you know who He is. Are you exasperated with life because nothing is working right? That may mean you're not doing it like He did it (and/or does it). Jesus came to save what was lost. When we lost our mindset, we lost our identity. Jesus—God in flesh and the second Adam all rolled up in one—came to save those who were lost. He purchased back our very souls and our identity.

You have the DNA to be just like God—not as the ruling deity of the universe but just like Him in His nature, methods, and emotions. When we fail to live up to this genetic code, the Bible calls it sin. Sin simply means to miss the mark or the pattern of who He is. While this sin the Bible talks about can be done out of rebellion and intentional disobedience, I believe it is mostly out of ignorance. Ignorance is defined as "lacking in workable knowledge." I believe too many people do not have a basic working knowledge of who God is, so they are lost.

We must go back to God's original blueprint. Within its pages, we will see a clear design of who God is and therefore a clear design of who we are. As we see the model of who He is and intentionally build our house after the same pattern, we will begin to see why God said we could subdue the earth, rule, and be very fruitful in life.

Chapter 15

Created to Create

The stage was set. Everything during six *yoms* of creation led to this moment. God scooped up the dust of the earth, formed the first human being, and blew the breath of life into him. God's first statement about this new species goes like this: "Let us make man in our image, in our likeness" (Gen. 1:26). The next verse reads, "So God created man in His own image, in the image of God he created him; male and female He created him." Within these first two sentences about man, God has reiterated four times the most essential information man would ever need to know about himself: he is made in the image and likeness of God. Man is the first clone of creation that was pulled from the very genetic code of who God is.

The knowledge that we were made like God is the only information God gave us upon our birth just prior to assigning us our great life mission of ruling the earth. The first thing God chose to tell us about ourselves is that we are just like Him. Let's have some fun. If we put this thing in reverse and back up to the start of this whole story in Genesis 1:1, the Bible says, "In the beginning God created the heavens and the earth." The first thing we know about God is that He is a Creator. God—the true author of this book we call the Bible—chose this information to be the first thing He told us as He introduced Himself to creation. The first thing we know about God is that He's a Creator; therefore, the first tangible thing we learn about man is he is a creator also.

I think it's important to believe that if God really is the God of creation, one of His greatest accomplishments was His ability to have the Bible written, collected, translated, and preserved in a perfect order so we can know His clear intentions for our lives. If that is so, it is only logical that God began His self-introduction in Genesis in a chronological order that was more than just historical but also spiritually instructive. If God tells us that we're like Him and then the first thing He tells us about Himself is that He's very creative—well, that's probably essential information. It seems to me that it was a priority for God that we know this about ourselves. In fact, God's assignment for man to subdue and exercise dominion over creation completely depended on it.

Just prior to writing this chapter, I took my family to Las Vegas as part of a fiftieth birthday present to my wife. I've flown many thousands of miles around the world through the years, but I found myself pondering this thing we call flight a little differently this time. Even with some knowledge of how all the aerodynamics of life and sustained flight work, I began to realize just how much we take for granted when we are cruising the heavens at thirty-two thousand feet and not dropping like a rock. The imagination, inspiration, and creative ability man has demonstrated in just this one area transcends far beyond what once seemed possible.

The fact is, that whole week in Las Vegas was quite the journey down memory lane because I was consistently reminded of the power and art of the universe's great creators. I was in awe more times than I could count as I viewed the collective creative genius of God and man. The Grand Canyon was breathtaking. The desert scenes and Red Rock Mountains were emotionally stirring. Those sights took me back to many other great masterpieces God painted, such as Niagara Falls and the great rainforests of Costa Rica. Only

God could create like that. I was also very impressed with what man had created. Nowhere in the world is there such a collection of great modern architecture in one place like in Las Vegas. The cutting-edge technology and media displays were thrilling and chilling. Goodness, there was even a TV built into the bathroom mirror at the hotel we stayed at. Could God create those things? Sure. But He didn't; man did, and it was impressive. But it was not just impressive to me as a man. I think God is impressed as well.

I can remember very vividly growing up in church and as a child, hearing preachers quoting Old Testament verses about the "increase of knowledge in the earth" and presenting it in a very negative light. However, I think our Father looks upon His children and is proud of our accomplishments. Sure, much of what we create can be used for good or evil, but that doesn't take away from the fact that even in our carnal nature we demonstrate a reminder that we are just like God in our ability to create. It's true—a TV in the bathroom mirror can't quite compare with the Grand Canyon. Maybe to God it's equivalent to my daughter's art that ends up on the front of my refrigerator. But maybe—just maybe—He really is impressed with it and wonders what we're going to imagine and create next. I thought it was quite interesting that our Grand Canyon tour also included a stop at Hoover Dam. I thought it was very appropriate that a tour that included the handiwork of the Father also included that of His sons.

As I sat pondering on our flight home, the 737 jet I was flying on no longer just seemed to be transportation. I began to see it as the fulfillment of God's original command to humanity to rule in the triune parts of earth. Dominion was to be exercised in the air, where the birds flew, in the seas, where the fish swam, and on the land, where the beasts of the field crawled. With each new generation comes an incredible increase in man's potential, which is expressed primarily through his creative ability. *It is not evil! It is like God!*

How corrupt it is that we stand in pulpits ushering humanity into an endless abyss of manmade godliness teachings. There is an eternal list of don'ts. Not doing the things God doesn't do makes us no more like God than the man in the moon. It is through the conforming to the image of *being like* God that leads us to great life, fruitfulness, joy, peace, and power. *Nothing* is more *like* God than tapping into the creative nature He placed within us.

We have exhausted ourselves in the body of Christ as we attempt to attain a manmade godliness. The more we try, the more we fail. It's one of the reasons why a whole century of the church fell into such an escape mentality in the twentieth century. The attainment of godliness was too elusive and ultimately condemning. You can only spiritually fail so many times in life before you lose heart and just want it all to end. But the true godliness that the Bible teaches is not labor intensive. It's not about trying to do or be anything other than who you are, which should be quite natural. We have become human beings who have forgotten we just need to *be*.

You, by nature, are a creator. You, by nature, have the ability to problem-solve and invent solutions to life's dilemmas. You are like the Marines—wired to improvise and adapt. You were born with a MacGyver spirit. All that dude needed was a paperclip, some used chewing gum, and a ballpoint pen, and he could take over a small country.

Regardless of the venue of life—marriage, parenting, finances, business, inventions, entrepreneurship, relationships—you are designed to take your world and improve it through the creative ability that is within you. You have the God-given power to create wealth and change your world. The first God wanted you to know about Him was that He's a creator. It's the first thing that God wanted you to know about yourself too.

Chapter 16

The Order of Artistry

Often at the start of a Sunday-morning message, I ask the congregation if I can just talk to them for a minute before I officially begin my sermon. Sometimes you just need to throw some things out there that set the tone for what you're about to say so it can be processed correctly. In light of that, can I talk to you for just a minute? My biggest challenge while writing this book has been the dilemma of giving you individual chapters of information that almost need a book by themselves to properly dissect, direct, and digest. I realize we all come from many different backgrounds, and the very concept of biblical foundations is an incredibly relative thing. Terminology that some find familiar may be very foreign to others. My intentional redundancy as a pastor with certain terms and statements in this book may grate on some while others are only understanding what I'm saying because of it. It can be tricky to introduce the spiritual side of Scripture to those only trained in the natural, and it can be even trickier to retrain the minds of those operating in the "super-spooky" realms of God to see Scripture on a very user-friendly level.

With that said, I need to tell you that every chapter of this book really cries out for you to become like the Bereans (Acts 17:11). If you want see what I'm trying to show you, you must go back and search Scripture for yourselves. I'm very intentionally attempting to take a whole new way of looking at the creation story and condensing it down to a rather short book. Ideally, this information would be best learned in a set of commentaries—but then you wouldn't be reading it right now, would you? Here's the thing: there are things I want to point out in a chapter like this that really could be books within themselves. The fact is that there are individual books that do talk about a lot of these things individually, yet I'm trying to collect all this information together so you can see God and His Kingdom in a more unified way.

The current topic is God's creative nature that has been passed on to us. This creative nature is in our DNA, which I have said stands for Divine Nature Acquired. But if this information goes beyond the theory realm and is tangible in our everyday lives, we can change what these familiar initials stand for. Divine Nature *Activated* is what God wants you to shoot for. For the creative power of God to become more than a concept and become an active part of your nature, we need to break down this process a little.

I think it's important for us to understand that before God ever began to create the first thing in Genesis, He clearly saw in His mind's eye what He wanted. It's called *imagination*. I'm not talking about the negative imaginations the apostle Paul talked about in 2 Corinthians 10:5. Those imaginations were the ones that are exalted *above* the knowledge of God. They were things outside the boundaries of God's truths. I'm talking more about what the Bible would probably call vision. The Bible clearly teaches us that without vision, God's people perish. The context of this statement is referring to the ability to see something that doesn't yet exist.

When I was a kid, my mom would always say, "Scotty, you have such an imagination." Sometimes that was a good thing and sometimes not. We only have this ability because we are a reflection of God. Long before God was the great Creator, He was the great imaginer. For how many *yoms* did God imagine and dream before He began to tangibly create all we see today? As a songwriter and a carpenter, I can really relate to this side of God. Long before anyone hears or sees the tangible side of what my hands create, my mind has seen at least the framework of the finished product. More of you than not who are reading this book can personally relate to this attribute.

The fruit that creative ability allows starts with pondering, dreaming, and imagining what we want to see that does not currently exist. If the creative process needs to be applied to my family, my job, a new business venture, or a new ministry idea, then it will always begin with pictures in my mind. We are often like David as we lie on our beds at night and meditate on life. Resolving conflict, problem-solving, and fresh ideas happen in the mind before they materialize in the flesh.

Today, we are living in a world that is exploding with advances in technology. All of these things that improve our world are things that have flowed out of a generation whose imaginations were intentionally cultivated. Most people who are my age know what is was like to grow up with a toy box mostly filled with sticks and rocks, but with applied imagination, wasn't it amazing what a stick could become? We became a generation of great inventors because of it. Today child psychologists are very concerned about a potential slowdown in technological advancement in the next generation. Instead of kids honing their own imaginations, they are spending most of their developmental time playing with someone else's imagination. Video games and TV consume the minds of our future inventors. While they play with what someone else imagined, their personal creative nature withers on the vine. The parents who told us to go outside and use our imaginations have mostly grown old or died. I fear some of our creative potential is going to the grave with them. They motivated us to think and in the process, inspired us to create.

God has given us all the ability to dream and imagine. It is out of this realm where we find the determination and inspiration to pursue and obtain. Nothing is created that is not first desired and hoped for. God dreamed. God imagined. It was the first stage of the creation process.

Imagination is one thing, but to actually create, you've got to have something to work with. If you imagine your dream house, you have to have material to work with if it's going to move from the unseen realm to the seen realm. It doesn't take much of deep mind to realize that, though, does it?

The problem is that, compared to what God obviously imagined at the start of creation, He really didn't have that much to work with. He imagined a finished work that would be breathtaking, to say the least. But how do you begin to create something so beautiful when all of your building material is formless, void, and covered with darkness? Well, guess what? This is not just be the story of God but of us also. I mean seriously, how often do you dream something really big, walk outside your front door, and suddenly find everything you need to work with sitting there in one big pile? The truth is that our supply usually doesn't parallel our dreams and imaginations. This is true in almost every venue of life. I want a better marriage, but I don't have what I need to work with. I want better finances, but I don't have what I need to get started. I want this dream of a new business, but where do I start?

Okay, let's start over. God said, "You're just like Me." In other words, how He did it is how you'll have to do it. He was showing us a pattern in real life. You dream and you imagine, but there doesn't seem to be much to work with. But God set the standard and showed us that if you have only a little supply but a whole lot of imagination, anything is possible. Throughout the Bible, He tells story after story of people who took what they had where they were at, got a little creative, and *voila!*

Five loaves and two fishes were enough when they were in the hands of a Creator. You want the greatest wine you've ever tasted, but all you have is water to work with? It's plenty when the DNA of God is on the scene. A slingshot in the hands of someone made in the image of God can turn an inconspicuous shepherd boy into an iconic hero. An ox goad is enough. A donkey's jawbone is enough. What have you imagined? What's in your hand? Get creative; it's enough.

God came to Moses and laid out an incredible ministry opportunity that would save millions. Moses heard the vision but couldn't see the possibilities.

"How can this be?" said Moses.

God said, "What's that in your hand, Moses?"

"Why, it's a staff," replied the simple shepherd.

"Throw it on the ground," God instructed.

When he did, it became a serpent, a living creature. God was sending Moses, as well as us, a message. If you will take what's in your hand and apply it to the earth, that thing you thought was a dead piece of wood has life in it. Pretty creative, huh?

God then added a third part to the creative process. He imagined what He wanted, took what He had to work with, *and started talking to it*. Into the dark chaos, God started talking about what He wanted. He began to demonstrate what He would later declare through King Solomon: "The tongue has the power of life and death, and those who love it will eat its fruit" (Prov. 18:21). From cover to cover, the Word of God redundantly reinforces this creative power that was put into play from the beginning. It's the pattern of God that has been echoed throughout the ages by prophets and apostles.

"When I am weak, I will *say* I am strong," declared the prophet Joel, along with the apostle Paul. The redeemed are instructed to *say* the things they know to be true as well as the things they hope for. We are made in the image of God. He is a God, the apostle Paul said, who "gives life to the dead and calls those things that are not as though they are" (Rom. 5:17).

I realize the instruction to "speak life" over our situations can be a very abstract and nondetailed tactic. I was raised in Pentecostal churches, where it was common to "speak life" over marriages, sickness, broken relationships, and derailed finances by saying, "I speak life over you." However, I want you to see that God was not so general with the words He spoke. He was actually trying to set a pattern in a way that would be very user-friendly and relatable. He simply began to change what did not exist into something He imagined by talking to it in the right way. It was not the words God spoke that are our pattern; rather, it is the fact that talking to creation the right way began to induce change.

Let's apply this to the areas of our world that may be in chaos. I want you to think about every venue of your life that is important. Think about your marriage, the relationship you have with your kids, and your job environment. For better or worse, the condition of each one of these sectors of your life is a response to one thing: *words*. It is not the challenges of life that destroy marriages. It is the words spoken when facing said challenges. Broken relationships between parents and children primarily exist because of words. Work environments are dictated by words. Friendships are formed and busted by words. Behavior patterns are a result of words that were dropped in the soil of people's lives from childhood—again, for better or worse. The list goes on and on. Chaotic, dark, depressed, formless, purposeless things in our lives are the harvest that has come forth from the seed we call words.

What God wanted you to see in His pattern of creation is that you can take all the broken stuff and make it productive and peaceful again simply by talking to it the right way. Hey, Charismatics, you got a little too deep on this one. I applaud all the prophesying and declaring you have been doing, but if you miss the simplicity that God was ultimately trying to show you … well, you pretty much missed 98 percent of the pattern. Rare would be the marriage that could not be made new if spouses would just start talking to each other in encouraging ways with a loving tone in their voices. In fact, rare would be any relationship or environment that could not be made new if we would just humble ourselves, change the tone of our voice, and start talking nicely to each other. The whole world could be transformed based on this one attribute God passed on to us faster than all other approaches combined.

God showed us how it works for Him so we would know how it would work for us. If you don't like your world, well, imagine how you really want it to be. Be content to take what you've got and start from there. Begin to talk to your world in ways that bring life, and not death. With each new day, things are going to start changing. Even on day one you will see your day getting brighter. If you keep talking to it in the right way, day by day, your life will start becoming what you dreamed of. What was dead will start coming back to life. What was producing no fruit at all will become productive. What started with chaos will end with a day of rest and peace.

Hey, American church! In this world you will have troubles. Remember, Jesus told you that so you would not be surprised. Marriage is tough; raising kids can be even harder. Some of you parents have probably figured out why some animals eat their young. Don't fret; God regretted having kids for a while too. He had to kick them out of the house and couldn't do a thing with them. Most of life is quite the challenge: money, relationships, jobs, entrepreneurial dreams, buying a house, keeping the car running, sending your kids to college … God knew all this. That's why He told us up front we would have to subdue the earth before we had dominion over it. But we can do it. How? We can do it by following the pattern of the one who made us.

God made it possible for nothing to be impossible for us … if we just believe. Believe what, that Jesus existed? No, we must believe we were created to be just like Him. He is the first fruits, and we are the harvest. Jesus did great things, and He said we would do even greater things. We are the sons of God. We carry the genetic code of the Creator of the universe, which means we are creators in the universe. No matter what the situation is, there's a solution. You've just got to get creative. No matter how limited your resources are, whatever you have is enough to start with. Just get creative.

Stop waiting on someone else to rescue you or bail you out. For most of you, there's not going to be *that* check in the mailbox tomorrow. It's not the government's job to take care of the sons of God. Stop scapegoating and waiting for *someday*, and imagine what you want. Take what you've got where you're at, and start talking to people in a way that brings life. Maintain that holding pattern, and over time, that thing that was not will be.

By the way, pastors, stop using most of the people's tithe money to buy things your congregations can produce with a little creativity. You may be shocked by what a few hundred dollars and a whole lot of imagination can do to transform a church and its ministry. Trust me, for some of us, it's the *only* option we have … and that ain't a bad thing at all!

Chapter 17

Canceling the Jerry Springer Show

The first time I saw it, I thought it was a joke. In fact, even though I never really saw a whole episode, I saw enough as I flipped through the channels to have a good idea of what was going on. It was the biggest collection of drama and dysfunctionality I had ever witnessed. It was called *The Jerry Springer Show*, and I just assumed anything so discombobulated had to be scripted. There was no way human beings actually lived like that in real life. Well, after many years of pastoring, I have some bad news: I was wrong. The show actually portrayed real life, though the word life is probably not be the best term to use here.

I have personally witnessed, counseled, and often been thoroughly depleted of energy by people who would make great guests on Jerry's show—families and individuals alike whose lives revolve around drama to the point of insanity. I've got to tell you, every square inch of my soul is repulsed by such a lifestyle. I'm not saying God hasn't given me the grace to patiently and lovingly help deliver folks from such a pit, but ministry aside, that chaotic world of recreational strife grates against my nature.

The reason I feel this way is simple: I am just like my Father. It was passed on to me through His DNA. Of course, I'm talking about my heavenly Father, in whose image you and I were made. This hatred of drama that is part of our spiritual genetic code was supposed to be so understood, that it was, in fact, the second thing God showed us about Himself. God hates *The Jerry Springer Show!*

All right, it wasn't called *The Jerry Springer Show* back when God was creating the world. But the Bible did a pretty detailed job in Genesis 1:2 describing a similar situation. Earlier I explained the meanings of the Hebrew words of Genesis1:2, which paint a vivid picture of creation's starting point. It was formless, it was empty, it lacked purpose, it was *chaotic*, and darkness covered it all. Let me use a more modern-day term that we might be able to relate to. Whatever this matter was that existed before God began the creation week, it was *dysfunctional*. There was no rhyme, reason, or purpose to it. It had no functional framework whatsoever to be productive or fruitful. It was just a big mess.

The second thing God chooses to show us about Himself is that He hates that kind of world. He has no use for dysfunctionality that holds no purpose or ability to produce life. His first action in creation was an intolerant rejection of such a world and a proactive stance to change it.

God's nature despised chaos and confusion, and we are made in His image. The call of godliness on our lives now demands we adhere to His nature and turn away from a carnal nature that is just the opposite of His. This action of turning away is what the Bible calls *repentance*. It begins with a revelation of *how* God is and an intentional will to conform to it. It requires us to die to our fleshly nature so His nature can resurrect in us.

Years of pastoring has taught me to not take too many things for granted when it comes to people's mindsets, so allow me to be very clear here regardless of how you grew up and what kind of patterns you've seen modeled. Humans do not get the right to decide what is considered *normal* when it comes to human behavior. That right is reserved for the inventor of the product: God. He defines what is normal and what is abnormal. With God, it's pretty simple; normal means to be like Him or to be *godly*.

With that said, it is important for you to understand that all this drama, confusion, chaos, and dysfunctionality going on in so many Christians is ungodly. This soap opera lifestyle we now accept as normal is *not* normal in the body of Christ. In the secular world, sure, but we are not of this world. While the world has become quite entertained by the drama queen she is, God is repulsed by it. How can we possibly be seeking the Kingdom of God for our lives and seeking recreational chaos at the same time?

It is to the Christian, the follower of Jesus Christ, who Paul exhorts to pursue godliness. It is the redeemed child of God who he challenges to become an imitator of Christ. We may have repeated a sinner's prayer and be a member in good standing in a local church. We may be covered with the blood of the Lamb and be assured of our place in eternity. But we may also be ungodly, which might explain why we've seemingly accomplished all of the above-mentioned protocols but are still lacking a fruitful life.

The second thing God showed us about Himself was that He hated a world of chaos, confusion, drama, and dysfunctionality. If we take on the same nature, we have taken a giant step on this journey of godliness. If we are "saved" but our lives are consumed with Jerry Springer theatrics, we are ungodly, and our lives will never yield the fruit the Bible promises. Jesus made clear in John 15 that these unfruitful branches would have to be cut off and thrown into the fire.

So, how's your marriage, your household, your many other relationships, your job, your church? Are they filled with drama? The nature of God is to despise it and become intentionally proactive to change your personal world into a life that will produce fruit and be filled with peace. You were designed by the Architect of Eden to be the exact same way. Hate chaos; love life.

Chapter 18

A God of Good Government

The Architect of Eden stands upon the building site of creation surveying the chaos and darkness before Him. He unrolls a blueprint that reveals on the first page the artist's rendition of the finished project. It's incredible! God's plan for the world is the most opposite thing a mind could ever imagine when comparing it to its state as He began creation. The plans called for the chaos to be replaced with harmonious systems of complex eco-balance. The darkness would be replaced by a diversity of beautiful lights that would color the heavens like an artist's canvas. The emptiness would be filled with a cornucopia of imaginative life forms, and the dysfunctionality would be retired by the motion of perpetual harvest. What a vision. What a plan. Let the construction begin!

If God is truly God, He could have wiggled His nose, said abracadabra, or simply sneezed in the right direction and produced this finished concept in an instant—but He didn't. He took six *yoms*—six periods of time—that very methodically staged His construction project. Day one set the stage for day two. Day two paved the way for the construction of day three and so on. There was a precise order to the days of creation, just as there is a precise order to the construction of a house.

If God didn't *have* to do it that way but chose to anyway, it tells us something incredibly important about Him. His nature is a nature of *order*. There is method when recreating madness into life. Things have to be done a specific way and in a specific order. If you start with a mess, it won't change overnight or by addressing it any old way you want. The "ordered steps of God" the psalmist talked about are what produces abundant life.

Earlier in the book, we talked a little bit about this nature of God. We saw how God displayed His character all through the Bible in different construction projects. Noah's Ark, Moses' Tabernacle, Solomon's Temple, and the New Jerusalem are all evidence of the architectural order of God. Through the person of Jesus, we see this nature identified in the Son of a Carpenter who builds the body of Christ methodically. The apostle Paul describes God's intentional style of construction, painting clear pictures of One who builds from the cornerstone and then lays the stonework of apostles and prophets followed by pastors, teachers, and evangelists. It's one of the first things we see about God. He is a God who takes things that are dysfunctionally out of order and turns them into something functional simply by restoring order.

Adam's primary sin was, in fact, the rejection of God's order. When he chose to eat from the tree of knowledge of good and evil, he was choosing his order over God's. His choice began to quickly return chaos and emptiness to a world God had made perfect. His life of peace was turned into a life of struggle and labor. His garden of perfect harmony began producing thorns, and the promise to be potentially fruitful was filled with pain. Man was out of order, and the price tag would be death on multiple levels.

The creation story paints vivid pictures of the beautiful life ordered by God and a dismal life when ordered by man. The generations of stories in the Bible only remind us of the chaos of man's condition when he is walking outside of God's ordered steps for humanity. But thank God, the story doesn't end there. The blueprint of God that started in a Garden of Eden picks back up in a Garden of Gethsemane four thousand years later. Isaiah prophesied that a Messiah was coming, and when He comes, His government would be on His shoulders, arriving with Him (Isa. 9:6–7).

Government may mean a lot of things to us, but in the original context, it simply meant *order*. It represented the order of how things would need to be in a society for it to be functional. Isaiah continued, "Of the increase of His government and peace there will be no end." In other words, He would re-implement what His Father, the chief carpenter and architect, originally ordered, with seasonal increase. Isaiah said an increase of His government would also lead to an increase of peace. It's probably no allegorical coincidence that an increase of God's order at creation led to a seventh day of rest and peace.

When Jesus began His ministry at thirty years of age, the gospels testify that He came preaching one primary message: "The Kingdom of God is at hand." The word "kingdom" was synonymous with "government." Time after time, Jesus would address people concerning what it would take to see or enter this kingdom of God or kingdom of heaven, depending on which gospel you are reading. It was clearly His primary thrust of ministry. He came announcing the re-implementing of God's order and then died on the cross to reopen the path to obtain it.

The Bible speaks of the veil that obstructed the Most Holy Place in the temple being ripped open when Jesus died, and it is very powerful imagery. This veil was decorated with embroidery work of a cherub holding a fiery sword. It was the reminder of the cherub with a flaming sword God placed to guard the entrance to the Garden of Eden when Adam was cast out. The work of the cross reopened the way to the place where God dwelled, and the place where God dwells is the place where God orders the steps of man's life.

Now you know something else about God, so you know something else about yourself. God is a god of order, which means if you are like God, your nature has to also pursue order. To pursue godliness means to pursue order for your life. To live haphazardly, with no purpose or function, is ungodly. If you are like Him, you can look chaos and dysfunctionality in the eye, and with some time and order, restore it into something beautiful.

With that said, let's make this thing a little more user-friendly. Take any important area of your life: marriage, family, money emotional health, fruitfulness—the list goes on and on. God's Word addresses every area of life that is essential to us. In every one of those areas, God gives us an order to how it works productively and functionally. God gives us an order to marriage. There is a man and a woman, and the two become one by leaving their parents. The man must love his wife like Jesus loves the church, and the woman must submit to her husband like the church should submit to Christ. Skip any of those ordered steps and the thing falls apart. We can go to every marriage seminar out there, but if we are missing the pages of the blueprint God designed, we are usually wasting our time.

Take money, for instance. God said to *first* (day one) bring the tithe into the storehouse, and then He will rebuke the devourer and open the windows of heaven over us. The story of Cain and Abel demonstrates this promise as Abel brought from the first fruits of his flocks and Cain brought from the leftovers of his harvest. God favored one and rejected the other. Abel was in God's order; Cain was not. So, my dear charismatic friends, we can speak to the four corners of the earth all day long saying, "Money cometh," but if we are out of God's order with tithing, ain't nothing coming but frustration. The good news is that if you will just order your steps after God's, then you don't have to add the specialty religious stuff. God said that if you get this thing in order, He will personally take care of the rest.

Okay, how about parenting? By the way, here's where I may finally make some of you hip psycho-analyzing parents mad. *God* is clear in His Word that there is an order in raising our kids. He holds dads responsible for teaching their kids about Him and His ways and also holds these same dads accountable to physically discipline his kids when they're *out of order*! Sure, we can try to impose our order on kids first, but as a pastor, I haven't seen it working out too well in most families.

Are you filled with worry, confusion, and depression? My first question has to be, are you doing the things God said would bring peace, joy, and a sound mind? Are you meditating on His Word? Do you have a prayer life? Are you in consistent fellowship where you can receive the corporate counsel of God? If you say no to these things, then your life is out of order. There is no bag full of spiritual abracadabras that will fix what your lack of order has broken. You can't override God's order with altar calls and the laying on of hands. You can't confess your way past it or even blame it on the devil. Hey, church, face it: our single biggest problem in life is one thing—*we are out if order!* If we get God's order back in our marriages, our families, our money, our time, our giftings, and our call, we will find life, fruitfulness, and finally some peace and rest.

You were made in the image of God. God said you can take any situation, no matter how messed up it is, and over time, turn it into something beautiful. It will require order, method, and patience, but it is in your DNA; it is in your nature.

Chapter 19

The Eternal Optimist

Do you want the life of God? Then you will only find it as you build a relationship with Him. There are no microwaves or get-rich-quick schemes in God's kingdom. However, there is a lot of confusion when it comes to this whole concept of "relationship with God." It sounds kind of abstract because can we humans really have what we call an intimate relationship with a spirit we only believe exists by faith? The answer is an emphatic *yes*, but let me give you an explanation of what I believe that means.

If the root of relationship is the word relate, then our connection to someone is based on the things we share in common. It may be anything from personality traits to life experiences. We share common beliefs, common hobbies, or common pasts. We share dreams and feelings that build connecting points in our souls. True relationship is a very tangible thing, not something elusive and abstract, so for me to have relationship with God, it means we have to share some things in common. God made the possibility of a relationship with Him easier than we think, starting with the first day of creation. He revealed things about His nature, His dreams, and His desires. He then made man and told him, "You're just like me." In other words, He wanted us to understand, right out of the gate, that there are all kinds of connecting dots that bond us together as we walk out our lives. As we embrace those bonds, it is like blood vessels flowing between the two of us. His life will flow into mine, and my life will flow back into His. This picture is the summation of all God wanted from the beginning.

Buuut! I know, here we go again with the big but. If we reject or rebel against the nature of God, we have, in fact, rejected the life of God. Churches are full of people who are doing all kinds of churchy things yet who struggle to find true life. But if we embrace the nature of God and willingly adopt it as our nature, then the promises of God will begin to automatically flood into our lives without sweat, tears, or labor.

Okay, American church, with that said, let me show you a primary nature of God we have to get back to—a part of who God is that we have rejected on a large scale. The first glimpse we get of this personality trait is in Genesis 1:4: "God saw the light was good, and He separated the light from darkness." I want to make sure you understand what is going on here. God has imagined something really good for this new world, but when He looks out His window, all 'He sees is a big, dark, chaotic mess. There's not much to work with, as the Bible speaks of much of the view as simply being emptiness. But God took what He had, where He was at, and began to speak life to it. By the end of day one, the only thing that changed was that the original mess was easier to see because of some light. Do you understand that the view wasn't necessarily all that improved in the first *yom* of God's creation process? Yet God looked at this very minimally changed view and had the audacity to say, *"This is good."* Wow, shouldn't He be kind of pessimistic that things didn't seem to be changing very fast?

Throughout the creation process, God (time and time again) views an unfinished project and has the ability to see the good that is happening all around Him. It becomes clear (early in the story) that God is an optimist. He had a very positive view of creation long before creation produced anything positive.

This optimistic nature is propagated throughout Scripture. Time and time again, God assigned incredible tasks to people who seemed to have little, if any, qualifications to complete said task. The one thread that became common with so many characters in the Bible is their "glass half-full" nature. Despite bleak conditions that set the environment of so many Bible stories, God found people who can see past the gloom and despair. While many stories contained cynics and great pessimists, they were never the heroes of the Bible. They were never the ones presented by God or Sunday school teachers hundreds of years later as the patterns for life.

No story of Scripture portrays this beautiful commodity of God's nature more than our first introduction to two spies named Joshua and Caleb. Moses sent twelve spies into Canaan to bring back reports of enemy strengths and the potential spoils of taking the land (Num. 13). Ten spies came back with despairing stories of adversarial challenges. "We can't do it," they cried. "We are grasshoppers in our own eyes."

But Joshua and Caleb stood up in the crowd with apparent confusion in their tone toward the other ten spies. "Of course we can do it!" they exclaimed. But the pessimism of the ten negative spies infected a whole culture, and a generation died in the desert, never obtaining the things God promised. It would be easy to make a case that the primary thing that separated those who entered God's promises from those who didn't was this optimism. Those like God— optimistic—got it all. Those who were ungodly—pessimistic—well, they got nothing.

Have you ever asked yourself why God chose a little boy like David to become the greatest king in Jewish history? We know God said it was because David was a man after God's own heart. But what does that really mean? Could it be that God saw David embracing this specific attribute of His nature? Could being a man after God's own heart simply mean we intentionally pursue those things that are natural to the heart and personality of God? David was an optimist, just *like* God. A whole army quaked in their boots as Goliath taunted them (1 Sam. 17). Little David walked onto the scene, looked past the size of the situation, and said, "Isn't he an uncircumcised Philistine?" Allow me the poetic license to paraphrase David's nature, words, and overall disposition more like this: "Sure, he's nine-and-a-half feet tall, is wearing 125 pounds of armor, has a spear with a fifteen-pound tip, and looks really scary. But *he's uncircumcised!* He doesn't walk in the favor of God!" Now, *that's* optimism: the ability to look past the worst and see the best.

As a pastor, I clearly see a dire need for this beautiful attribute of God's nature to be reattached to the body of Christ. How would everything from evangelism to church growth be affected if the sons of God could look past the bad and see the incredibly neat things happening in the earth? I'm sick of hearing about the good old days from the crowds of people who are clogging the arteries of Christ's body—people who are historically and theologically illiterate to the truths of man's history and the promises of our future, right here, right now. The reality is that there has never been a time when man has so prospered or the church so expanded in the earth. Sure, denominations may be shrinking, but that doesn't mean the church is not growing.

Not only are the numbers of people in the church swelling by the day, but revelation knowledge of God's Word is also exploding like no time in history. Yeah, there are still wars, plagues, and natural disasters, but if you stayed awake in junior high history, you know that the scale of these thorns in man's side is nothing compared to days gone by. Mind you, I'm not in denial concerning all the bad stuff out there, but I can also see positive things happening as in no other time in man's history. Economies have always been up and down. The Bible makes it clear that as long as we are in this age, there will be war on earth. There will always be starving people somewhere and crime will always exist, but these "tares" are not the signs of the times. Jesus taught us to keep our eyes on the wheat, and the wheat is growing beautifully as we head toward the great harvest.

I know the "positive thinking" trend has really taken off in America, even within the church, but the thought that this philosophy is a secular idea is pretty ludicrous. God, not Robert Schuller, is the Creator of this way of thinking and living. What secular psychologists confirm concerning positive thinking is simply the way God wired humanity from the very beginning. Optimistic people generally live longer, have less stress, have better control of their emotions, cope better with conflict, and are generally more content with their lives. Those who view life through a positive filter are more productive on their jobs, have more functionality in their families, and have much richer social lives. These examples just scratch the surface of the distinct advantages optimistic people seem to have in life.

It is a pessimistic nature that has caused much of the escape theology propagated in the twentieth-century American church. It has blinded us to the increase of God's Kingdom and the progression of God's image in humanity. God's people have once again become filled with a griping, murmuring spirit that complains about everything, as well as negative mindsets that see no hope for future generations. These are minus-mouth Christians whose pastime is to degrade our spot in history and our position as the sons of the living God.

Nothing has changed in the realm of God, however. The Old Testament stories are pictures of our spiritual reality, as the apostle Paul declared, and the redundant message is clear. Optimistic children of God enter into a land filled with God's glorious promises. Pessimists die in dry, barren places as they wander around in circles.

Pessimists can't see what's right in front of them. Even the Moses generation seemingly could not see that they were surrounded by most likely thousands of livestock as they complained to God they were hungry. Negative folks would never see the possibilities of five loaves and two fishes or a slingshot. People who only see the bad in life will seldom become great creators, inventors, or entrepreneurs. While optimists plow into the future with great hope and enthusiasm, pessimists sit around doing nothing while they wait for someone to just come rescue them.

Let me make this simple: God is the great eternal Optimist. That is His nature. We were made in His image. To become godly means we must also take on that nature. To have a pessimistic nature is to be ungodly or dare I even say, anti-Christ. I say that because the nature of Jesus was obviously not only King of kings, but He was also clearly King of the optimists. He came preaching a positive gospel that was supposed to bring *life* to people, not despair. To follow Him as His disciples requires that we take on His attitude. To become this corporate harvest the Bible calls the church means we must mimic His persona.

God said it was good before it really was. How do you view life?

Chapter 20

Father Time

Let's pose a valid theological question: does God wear a watch? "Silly," you say, but let's look at the evidence of Scripture. Just five sentences into the story of God's nature and man's origin, we see God is measuring time. Verse 5 of the first chapter of Genesis says, "God called the light 'day' and the darkness he called 'night.' And there was evening, and there was morning, the first day." It's the first *yom* of creation, and we see that both a clock and a calendar have come into play. Remember, man has not been created yet, so this eternal God who would seemingly have no use for keeping track of time on any level ... is keeping time.

Out of the natural side of the Genesis story, creation was introduced to the concept of hours, days, weeks, and because of the evolving patterns of the sun, even the seasonal spans of a year. All of this was done before a creature existed that would even need to mark time. The surface argument would, of course, be that God was preparing the table for man's arrival, knowing he would need to operate within this structure. But the question is why? If God doesn't mark time, why would the man who was made in His image need to?

The answer to this question is found within the very actions of God recorded in Genesis. There is clearly an active agenda of God that staircases in increments from the start of God's building project until its completion. God is marking what He is doing, just as any architect's proposed timeline for construction would do today. God is framing His daily accomplishments. Within the historical report of God's finished days is a record of achieved goals and checkmarks on the daily to-do list. God's days are a report of fruitful and productive ventures that have longevity in the days and years to come. It is the story of time well-spent doing things that mattered and were not a waste of time. It is the perfect introduction to the concept of a "purpose-driven life."

The first 25 verses of Genesis 1 are about God, how He operates, and what He is *like*. In verse 26, man is created in the *image* and *likeness* of God. Isn't it interesting that within the few sentences in which God introduces us to Himself, a spotlight is shining on His time-management skills? His nature really is that as Father Time, giving us an in-your-face glimpse of what it is we are supposed to be like. Managing the accomplishments of a day was priority to Him and therefore is to be a priority to us also.

Once again, the messages of early Genesis are now replicated in redundant form through the rest of God's Word to us. Great emphasis on *time* is placed within the framework of almost every Bible story. We see the great adventures of God and man told within the boundaries of generations, years, months, days, and hours; success and failures following the path of timelines; kings and their kingdoms; and prophets and their prophecies all operating within the structure of calendars, clocks, and construction timelines.

This attribute of God's nature once again reminds us that you can't remove a single component of how God is from our DNA and expect the results the Bible has promised us to be realized in our lives. We can be creative, optimistic, and hungry to produce good fruit in our lives, but if we don't manage our time correctly, then we become as the grass of the field Moses spoke of in Psalm 90:6. In the morning, we spring up, but by evening we are dry and withered.

In other words, life is over before you know it, which is why Moses continued in this great Psalm to say, "Teach us O Lord to number our days aright." This is coming from a man who spent forty years of life wondering around in circles in a dry, barren wasteland, never entering the place God promised.

The apostle James understood the speed of life and described it as a mist that rises with the morning and then quickly dissipates. He exhorts us to make sure we are spending our days seeking the will of God and not our own fruitless endeavors. The apostle Paul challenges us to make sure we are not running around aimlessly, like a man beating the air. Jesus provokes us to lay our treasures up in heaven where moth and rust can't destroy. We have redundant direction from God that reminds us to be *like him*—a shrewd manager of the time we have been given.

Few things irk me more as a pastor than continually watching people who are heavy-laden with gifts, talents, and abilities who do nothing with them. Oh, they are always planning on it—*someday*. Too much of the body of Christ has put the "pro" in procrastination as we sit waiting for a better time or place to realize the dreams and desires God has put in our hearts. We labor in life to find our day of rest because we never actually finish the labors of the day. Nothing will emotionally, spiritually, or even physically exhaust a person more than the continual haunting of unfinished tasks. Failing to complete your dreams and goals of life leads to discontentment that is often wrongly assigned to many other scapegoats. We wake up tired before we ever start our day because our lives are burning by and we are not accomplishing the things of life we know are important. We labor, never finding our Sabbath or a season where we can truly rest and relax our mind and spirit.

I've searched everywhere I know to look, and I can't seem to find the brake on this thing. I can't slow life down, so I must revert back to the original blueprint to find the breakdown in the system. God started a day, labored, finished, and then said, "This was good."

That is not just supposed to be the story of God but my story too. I realize that to find goodness in my days, with rest at the end of my week, I must be able to look back at those days that flew by and see that I accomplished some good, meaningful things. I can't slow life down, but I can look in the rearview mirror and rest knowing that my days have mattered in how I have lived them. I haven't spent them procrastinating or simply being lazy with my dreams.

God gave us the blueprint. The abundance in life Jesus promised is found within the framework of proper labor that is followed by proper rest. This pattern of God's nature allows for recreation and fun, but it is also a pattern that reminds us of how we are wired. We are wired to be discontent if we are not living a purpose-driven life. For those who want more details on that, go buy Rick Warren's book, *The Purpose-Driven Life*. It will inspire you to become more intentional with how you are spending your days.

Okay, so here we have it again—an attribute of God that, when mimicked, will bring great life. I know time-management skills don't seem all that spiritual, but that's only because most of us grew up in churches that spent most of their time telling us what *not* to do instead of *how to be like God*. The abundant life Jesus promised us is found in godliness or conforming to the very image of God. God finished His days and said they were good. We're finishing our days with few good things to say. We've got to get back to the blueprint. We must reflect this dire attribute of God. It is *the* missing link that so many talented, gifted Christians have missed. Reconnect this one wire, and see if it doesn't radically transform your days into something fruitful, productive, and *good*.

Chapter 21

Lord of the Harvest

Early in the creation process (on day three, in fact) God began to reflect what could be the most pivotal peek into His nature. He created vegetation, building into its systems the ability to perpetually reproduce. God is detailed concerning the production of seed and fruit; these plants had to be able to provide something of value in their current state, as well as produce a legacy beyond themselves. On days five and six, God would mirror this personality trait with the creation of birds, fish, and creatures that crawl on the ground, as well as humankind itself. The proclamation of God over these living creatures would hold the command to be fruitful, multiply, increase, and fill the earth. Within these terms lie the purpose of the labor we discussed in the last chapter. God is driven by being productive in life, and He expects those made in His image to follow suit.

Literally, from the first chapter of Genesis to the final chapter of Revelation, God deals with fruitfulness. His story begins in a garden filled with fruit-bearing trees and ends in a garden filled with fruit-bearing trees. Whether the Garden of Eden in Genesis or the New Jerusalem of Revelation, the picture is the same: God's world is a world of production. It's one of those more common, recurring themes of the Bible. Throughout the Bible there are pictures of fruit trees, gardens, and even Jesus Himself being mistaken for a gardener after His resurrection … in a garden. By the way, that was not a mistake; God *is* the gardener. Jesus said Himself in John 15:1, "I am the vine, and my Father is the gardener." He followed that statement by one of His most important commentaries to humanity concerning God's will for their lives, which was *producing fruit!* In fact, all of this imagery of cutting off unproductive branches, the Refiner's Fire, the Winepress, and the Potter's Wheel is about one thing: putting humankind in a place of being fruitful with their lives. Holiness, which we dealt with earlier in this book, is about one thing: producing fruit. Walking with God is confirmed by two things: loving one another and producing fruit. We need to produce fruit right now where we currently are—and as Jesus added, fruit that will last. He was speaking of seed that would continue to reproduce after its own kind just as God designed for every living thing on earth.

In John 15:16, Jesus said, "You did not choose me, but I chose you and appointed you to go and bear fruit; fruit that will last." He was echoing the original command of God to man in Genesis 1:28, "Be fruitful and increase in number; fill the earth and subdue it." It is the first order of God's will for man, echoed by Jesus, and taught by the apostles. It is the grafting point, according to Jesus, to the very heart of God. It is the tangible side of knowing God, walking with Him, and being about His business.

God reveals His heart and mind and then makes us in His image. His nature is a world driven by increase and multiplication. It's a world filled with fruitful living that carries into generations that follow. It's a personality trait expressed in the DNA of His very kingdom that, according to Scripture, is ever-expanding and has no end to its enlargement capabilities. It's a lifestyle of inspirations and motivations driven by the desire to be fruitful now and beyond our years.

Now you know why God expresses disdain through the writers of the Bible for lazy and slothful people. Busybodies that are not constructive in God's kingdom are rebuked, and religious people holding back production are cast in a very negative shadow. God wants us to get it: we are His seed and seeds reproduce.

So where is all of this fruitfulness supposed to be expressed? Well, in the tangible world we all live in every day—in our families, our workplaces, our neighborhoods, and the ministries expressed through our local churches. It's all supposed to take place in the same world Jesus lived in where we eat, work, shop, worship, and recreate. We produce fruit in how we raise our kids, love our coworkers, and labor for those who are kind enough to hire us. We produce an increase that can leave a legacy when we utilize the gifts God has wired into our individual DNAs and share the skill sets we've developed over time. When we take our experiences in life, bad and good, and use them to help make someone else's life better, we are being fruitful. When we bring a tithe of our income that we have labored so hard for into God's storehouse to be used in the ministries of the local church, we are bringing increase to God's kingdom. When we feed a hungry person, help clothe the newborn baby of a family who has little, or simply take time to counsel a confused teenager, we are dropping seed that, over time, can yield a harvest.

God made His nature clear from the beginning. He has a *harvest* attitude in how He views and approaches life. If we want to be godly, we must take on this same attitude. With this attitude comes the promise of great blessings, insights into God's counsel, and a supernatural ability to garner the promises of God. God did not make you to be a spectator. He made you to be a player who is in the game and highly inspired to win. If church to you is a spectator sport, you are ungodly. You are not *like* Him. If you are not *like* Him, then you will not like what life becomes for you.

I encourage you to keep this thing simple. Don't condemn or overwhelm yourself with this exhortation of fruitfulness—*but* get in the game. You will find this yoking with God's nature to be easy. In fact, it leads to rest. Stop being a busybody, and get busy being about your Father's business. Stop exhausting yourself producing things that rust and that moths can destroy, and make your body a living sacrifice to labors that are worship unto God. Stop being just a taker, and become the reflection of the One who is the giver of life. In the words of John the Baptist, "Produce fruit in keeping with your repentance" (Luke 3:8).

Chapter 22

Finding the Finish Line

As I wrote this book, my wife turned fifty. My gift to her was a stay at the Trump Tower in Las Vegas for a few days of rest and recreation. The gift within the gift was some spa time where she was rubbed, scrubbed, and dubbed a queen for a day. My wife works hard at her job, with long hours and some weighty responsibility. Her labors earn her the right to special days of rest. This gift for my wife merely models the original design God drew up in His blueprint for man.

Genesis 2:2 says, "By the seventh day God had finished the work He had been doing; so on the seventh day He rested from all His work." What a wonderful attribute of God—a desire to *rest*. He is a God who has set forth a pattern for perfect harmony in life: productive work followed by productive rest. We, of course, follow this natural pattern in our everyday lives as we generally work five to six days a week and rest one. In the old days, Sunday was the universal day of rest. That, of course, has sadly changed for many.

But it's so important for us to see past the natural part of this pattern and understand the deeper issues of how rest has been wired into our DNA. We need to see that for God, rest was not simply taking a day off; it was an emotional contentment due to a completed agenda. Genesis 2:2 clearly precedes rest with the acknowledgment of finished work. This finished work was the culmination and fulfillment of every single component of God's nature we have discussed in the past few chapters. This "finishing" held the ingredients of vision, imagination, creativity, order, optimism, time management, and fruitfulness. Before God could rest, some things in His heart had to be brought to fruition. Before He could take a deep breath and kick back in the hammock, He had to look back and know He had put into motion His dreams and talents. Rest for the soul would not simply hinge on the workweek being over but on a retrospect of fruitfulness and satisfied accomplishments.

The Sabbath rest God speaks of in Genesis is a realm where the whole man finds contentment and satisfaction with where life is going. Though presented through many cultures as a literal day where everyone should go to church, Hebrews 4 takes the story into deeper spiritual realms. We learn this Sabbath day of rest is not a literal twenty-four-hour day of the week but a place of spiritual living in a New Covenant. It's a picture of a priesthood wearing linen undergarments, which spiritually denotes labor without the sweat of human endeavor. It's a place we *enter* through the gate of Christ Jesus. But the gate leads to the restoration of a kingdom—an order whose components culminate into a great life of fruitfulness followed by rest. It's a world where our vision, creativity, optimism, and time management are processed through the Spirit of God that dwells within us. When combined in this way, our labors do not drain and demoralize us. In fact, they invigorate and revitalize us as we restfully look back on the fruit that was produced. We become the burning bush of God, always on fire but never consumed (Ex. 3).

As I mentioned in a previous chapter, nothing can drain a person like unproductive labor where we are always working hard at life but never truly finishing our dreams and goals. I have always said that dreams and vision are the zest of life, but if they go unrealized for too long, they can end up choking the very life out of us. We see from God's nature that He is a finisher. Jesus, the Author and Finisher of our faith, reminded us of this nature as He completed His purpose in the earth. *"It is finished!"* He declares from Calvary's cross (John 19:30). He had pushed through the adversity and opposition of life to accomplish all His Father had set before Him. Now He would rest as He returned to sit at the right hand of His Father.

I would be afraid to guess at the percentage of time I spend in the counseling chambers with individuals who are sick at heart in life, only because they are exhausted from never finishing the things they put their heart and hands to. They may take their days off from their jobs but never really find the rest their souls so desperately need. For Christians who fit this description, one of the first places we need to investigate is our personal to-do list in life. If we are not looking back at day one, day two, day three and finishing those days with, "It was good," then our day of rest may never come. Oh, but finish some projects, meet some goals, and sow a little servant time, and watch how quickly the sandman does his work when you lay down to sleep. You can wake up on your day off ready to enjoy your family and the simplest things life can offer.

It is in God's nature to finish those things that are immediate in His heart and then enter a *yom* of rest. We are to reflect this image in our everyday lives. Sure, some days are more productive than others; we even have days that seem to accomplish nothing (or even worse, where we suffer loss). *But* we must still stay in the mindset of intentionally finishing the things that matter so we can enter the true rest of God—rest that re-energizes the body, soul, and spirit. It's simple math. Imagine it, create it with optimism, manage your time wisely, and finish it … and then *you will enter rest.*

This is God's blueprint for your life. It is the order of His kingdom. It is His will that you prosper in fruitfulness and live a Sabbath lifestyle. He doesn't want your race in life to be in vain but rather wants you to find reward in it, as the apostle Paul did. God's plan for your life is that your labors lead to rest, not debilitating emotional and spiritual exhaustion. Follow His lead. Finish what you started, and enter His rest.

Chapter 23

The Clone of God

So God created man in His own image, in the image
of God He created him; male and female He created
them. God blessed them and said to them, "Be fruitful
and increase in number; fill the earth and subdue it."
(Gen. 1:27–28)

It always amazes me how often I see the natural realm we live
in reflect and mimic the spiritual processes of God. Sometimes
it happens without much notice at all, even though it may be a
monumental event. In 1996 when Dolly became the first cloned
mammal, most people just watched from a distance through the filter
of science. Many Christians, of course, were up in arms debating
the ethics of such a process and wondering if mankind had crossed
a line, but Dolly held my attention in a way that created a whole
new category of clone observers. As I watched the process unfold,
I couldn't help but think, *Gee, I've seen this before.* Mankind was
attempting to somehow duplicate the greatest creative miracle of
God.

The fact is, no matter how you slice this thing, Adam was the
first official clone of creation. Out of His own DNA, God pulled
from Himself the substance that, over time, would turn into a being
that would be just *like* Him. It is interesting how quickly the church

pronounced judgment over a process that technically originated with God. Mankind—regardless of your ethical stance on cloning—was simply following God's lead. It's pretty ironic that Dolly just happened to be a sheep, isn't it? Of all the animals they could have cloned, they just had to grab a critter the Bible used to represent the children of God.

Look, I realize the jury is still out for many of us concerning this whole cloning thing, but don't get sidetracked by that. I'm trying to show you something much deeper here. Dolly was a product of some very small strands of DNA pulled from another sheep. As the process evolved, Dolly began to take shape and in time became a living, breathing creature. When the process was finished, Dolly looked exactly like the sheep whose DNA she was pulled from. Hear me now: Dolly was *not* the original sheep, but she clearly reflected what the original sheep looked like.

When God pulled from His nature the substance to create man, this man was supposed to turn into a being that would, over time, reflect the image of God. Understand that this man would never *be* God, but he certainly was supposed to be just like Him in His character and attitudes. God and man would resemble one another in their desires for relationship and their hunger for life beyond their own. Man would be a mirror into the very soul of God, reflecting personality traits and emotion. The skills and abilities of man would resemble the same attributes God would demonstrate all through the Bible. Man would be just *like* God.

Because man would be just like God in nature, he would therefore be just like God in his potential to operate in a position of dominion. As God completed the task of creating man, He prophetically decreed man's authority to rule in the earth. Everything God created, from the plants to the animals, was given to humans as the caretakers of the earth. Not just the seen but the unseen would have to submit to man's rule—assuming this man truly understood who he was. Jesus, the second Adam and Son of God, came to remind us of the first

Adam's potential. Everything from Mother Nature to the hordes of hell yielded to the voice of Jesus' command. He demonstrated the subduing power proclaimed over the first Adam, treading on every enemy to humanity. Whether sickness or demonic entities, Jesus exercised dominion power—a power whose right belonged not only to Him but also to all Adams who would yield their lives to the Kingdom of God.

Humans were created to be kings in the earth. Humans were preordained to be the head and not the tail. No weapon formed against them would prosper, and the gates of hell would not prevail against them. They would hold the keys to the very kingdom of heaven, and *nothing* would be able to stop them from conquering and lording over all God had assigned to them. The whole earth and the fullness thereof would not only belong to the Creator but also to the sons who would be seated in heavenly realms with Him.

We humans seem to only have one problem with this masterful design of God: *we don't believe it!* Sure, in theory we speak it, at least out of one side of our mouths. But out of the other side flows the cursings of those who have no idea of who they really are. We clamor for God to snatch us out of the very world we were given to subdue and rule over. Our escape theology and left-behind attitudes relegates our existence to those of slaves, not kings. We have a crippled, pauper mentality as we sit *outside* the gate called beautiful, holding up our little tin cups begging for enough morsels to get us through another day (Acts 3). In miracle after miracle in the New Testament, we see the picture of crippled people being pulled to their feet and told to walk. We see people being delivered from blindness and the inability to hear or speak. We see literal miracles that speak from deeper realms of God's agenda to open our ears to rehear the truth of just who we are, start walking like those made in His image again, and speak the words of life that can transform the world in which we live.

Our dirt-bag mindsets have become a cancer in the body of Christ, slapping the reinstating work of the cross right in the face. It has perverted our perspective of who we are and why we are here. Its gangrene effect has permeated the way we have church and even why we have it. I see it in how we pray—like beggars instead of sons of the living God. I see it in how we worship—like groveling sinners instead of kings. I see it in how we treat each other—like yesterday's trash instead of the family that links our destinies. Our minds are warped and must be renewed.

God, the eternal Creator and owner of the universe, pulled from His personal supply of DNA and made *you* in His image. The seed of His nature has been deposited in you from the time you were meticulously knit together in your mother's womb. From the time of your birth into this earth, the order of God's plan for your life is to take you through the process that turns the seed of His nature into a harvest of His nature. This process is what the Bible calls the Refiner's Fire, the Potter's Wheel, and the Threshing Floor; its stages of development are modeled by the Gardener trimming off unproductive branches so we can become fruitful. They are the works of God in our lives that process out under the biblical headings of *holiness* and *godliness.* As we undergo multiple stages of separation, we're just like the rocket that flies higher into the atmosphere. As we intentionally conform to the character of God, we begin to take on the life and power of God. It's simply called growing up.

This *is* who you are, regardless of all the dumb, stupid, wrong things you've done. Despite past rebellion and racing down a path of worldly living, you're never more than just a few renewed brain cells away from beginning to live the truth of who God made you to be. It doesn't take perfection; it only takes faith—faith to believe you *are* who God says that you are. Your sin? Well, it was forgiven two thousand years ago … if you can accept that. And not just your past sins, but all your future sins too … if you can accept that as well. If you can, it will set you free to pursue the destiny of who God made you to be instead of exhausting yourself trying to "stay saved."

We were created in the image of God, and from our original birth from God's womb, blessings have been pronounced over us. Genesis 1:28 says, "God *blessed* them ..." The word "bless" simply means "favor." From the beginning, humankind *has* been walking in the favor of the one who created them. Sure, the Bible is clear that it is obedience that leads to the blessings of God. But what does that mean—to be obedient to God? Simple! It means to follow the original blueprint the Architect of Eden drew up for us at the founding of creation—submission to works of holiness and godliness. It means cooperating with the Spirit of God to follow the *ordered steps* designed for us from the beginning.

The Architect who designed us has now become the Carpenter who builds us. His plan is simple but does take some faith to pursue. This faith becomes the daily actions of allowing a work in our lives that we believe leads to a life of abundance. It elevates us to a position of rule that brings great contentment to our lives. It gives us confidence that we *are* God's children, and our Father is absolutely *for us*. We may be flawed, but God's plan for us is not. Your design and all the great promises that come with it have been sealed by the one who loves you more than He loves Himself ... the Architect of Eden.